Contents

||| || ||||||||||| ||| ||| ||
W0013616

Preface

In writing the second edition of this book I wanted to put my experiences of the last 15 years on paper. The book has once again been thoroughly revised, this time taking into account guidance and information concerning the revisions made to the APC in July 2006.

This book is designed to help supervisors and counsellors who work to steer candidates into the profession. For you I have three words of advice: invest, invest, invest! Surveyors are not born fully formed, but are inspired, encouraged, trained and developed by a range of people over the course of their careers. During the period of structured training that constitutes the APC, the supervisors and counsellors carry out all of these functions. This book aims to help you understand the investment you, and your employers, must make, and to explain how you can get the best return on it.

From an APC perspective, the investment starts on day one of the training period. The rewards, for both the employer and the candidate, will quickly follow – my experiences based on my involvement with the APC over the years are proof of this. Good supervision and counselling, supporting a well-structured and focused training period, will turn the final assessment into simply a validatory process. On many occasions over the years, I have been approached by training managers who have proudly advised me of 100% pass rates at the last APC.

It doesn't stop there. The APC training period is the young surveyor's first impressions of our profession. Good first impressions will provide the true experts and leaders of the future. In the context of the APC – and of training generally – I am a zealot! I firmly believe that there is nothing more important, in terms of unlocking future potential, than a sound first couple of years of training and experience.

One of the most eye-opening periods of my career was in the early 1990s, when I was appointed to the role of training and development manager in the Valuation Office Agency. In this role I saw clearly how employees' true potential could be unleashed, and excellent business results delivered, by equipping members of staff to perform their jobs with confidence. I also saw the other side of the equation – the disastrous consequences that could occur when people were not properly trained. It was in this job that my early involvement with the APC began: teaching, training and supporting graduates in the early stages of their careers.

The business world we live in has changed considerably over my years in this field. Management best practice is now focusing heavily on training as an investment for the future – that is to say, the future of the company or business making the investment, as well as that of the employee benefiting from the training.

The APC is no exception. There will be a high expectation in the candidate's mind that the employer will deliver not just the appropriate training, but support and encouragement, both during the training period and final assessment, and in order to provide the foundations for a successful and rewarding career as a chartered surveyor. There will be an equally high expectation on the part of the employer that the candidate will rise to the occasion, go on to be a useful addition to the firm and the profession generally.

The commitment on the part of the employer also involves making an investment in the more senior people who will act as supervisors and counsellors for the candidate, and in training them to carry out this role satisfactorily. For supervisors and counsellors, the experience gained from carrying out the roles can be thought of as general management training, useful across the wider spectrum of staff appraisals, end-of-year reviews, and promotion and assessment generally. You may also like to consider all of the hours that will qualify for continuing professional development (CPD) purposes.

More importantly, supervisors and counsellors should derive a great sense of satisfaction from providing support to people in the early part of their career. Your satisfaction should grow as your trainees develop and progress, providing a great sense of achievement and reward. I would therefore urge employers, supervisors and counsellors to 'make the investment' and follow the guidance in this book – in order to deliver the talent of the future.

It must be stressed (and is repeated throughout the book), that the advice given is, except where noted otherwise, solely my own. I draw upon my own experiences as an APC trainer and assessor, and the experiences of the many people I have come into contact with over the 30 years I have worked as a chartered surveyor. This book is intended to complement – not to replace – the official guidance provided by RICS. The APC is a dynamic programme; it is constantly under review, as part of RICS' commitment to continuous improvement. Should any future changes result in discrepancy between the official APC guidance and the advice in this book, the official material should always take precedence.

While this book cannot *guarantee* success for candidates, it can at least point supervisors and counsellors to the *right way* to success – providing a helpful explanation of the various processes and documents, reminders of the requirements, and tips as to how to meet them, handy checklists of 'what to do when', and case studies to help you plan your own actions.

All current matters and developments regarding the APC are published on the RICS website (www.rics.org) or for further information contact the Membership Operations Department by email contactrics@rics.org, phone +44 (0)870 333 1600 or fax +44 (0)20 7334 3811.

Finally, I would like to thank all those members of RICS who have helped bring this book to fruition, with particular mention for Vivien Small, head of the RICS Education and Qualification Standards Department, and Sue Roberts of the RICS Membership Operations Department.

John Wilkinson

1. Introduction to the APC

To understand what is required of you as a supervisor or counsellor, an appreciation of some of the background philosophies and key concepts of the APC is vital. This chapter is mainly designed for those of you who are new to the process – however, even those more experienced at APC training should find it useful. The APC is a constantly developing programme and all those involved must ensure that they have an up-to-date knowledge of its requirements and concepts.

Let's start at the very beginning.

WHAT IS THE APC?

The APC is the RICS' Assessment of Professional Competence. It is the practical training and experience, which when combined with academic qualifications leads to RICS membership. It is first and foremost a period of structured training and further study, and is followed by a 'final assessment' of each candidate's knowledge, experience and work to date.

The APC is undertaken by candidates who have graduated with an RICS-accredited degree and who have commenced or are in relevant employment. Although supervisors and counsellors only play a role in Graduate

1

Routes 1 and 2, there are various 'routes' which will lead candidates to membership of RICS including:

- **Graduate Route 1** – for those with an RICS accredited degree and no professional experience, requires a minimum 24 months of structured training;

- **Graduate Route 2** – for those with an RICS accredited degree and five-years relevant experience (pre-degree experience counts), requires a minimum 12 months of structured training;

- **Graduate Route 3** – for those with an RICS accredited degree and ten-years relevant experience (pre-degree experience counts);

- **Adaptation Route 1** – for those with an RICS-approved professional body membership or non-accredited degree AND 450 study hours from an RICS-accredited degree either at postgraduate level or final year of an undergraduate programme or from an approved training provider;

- **Adaptation Route 2** – for EU applications, contacts RICS for more details;

- **Academic** – for those who are teaching or researching on an RICS accredited degree; and

- **Senior Professional** – for professionals who are now in a senior industry position.

The routes all culminate in attendance at a final assessment interview. Those who are successful at this interview gain professional status.

In essence, therefore, the APC is the process by which RICS seeks to be satisfied that candidates who wish to become members are competent to practice as chartered surveyors.

The assessment of competence is carried out over the full period of training or relevant experience – not simply at the final assessment interview. Supervisors and counsellors play a primary role in both the training and assessment of candidates.

The APC can be thought of in two parts:

● the structured training process;

● the final assessment interview.

STUDY AND LEARNING Which may take place at university	+	APC Two years (minimum) practical training and experience	=	MRICS Membership of RICS

The structured training process

The structured training process is rigorous and demanding. It takes place over a minimum period of 24 calendar months and includes a minimum of 400 days of relevant experience for Graduate Route 1 candidates or 12 calendar months and a minimum of 200 days for Graduate Route 2 candidates. The objective is to show that the knowledge and theory gained primarily in higher education is complemented with practical experience.

During the period of structured training, the candidate is expected to keep a record of experience gained in a diary. The candidate must also keep a log book, to include a record of professional development, and complete, along with the supervisor and counsellor, an achievement record. These documents, and the role of the supervisor and counsellor with regard to them, are discussed further in Chapter 5.

The final assessment interview

The final assessment interview is the second part of the APC process. A panel of a minimum of two assessors (the panel will normally comprise three assessors), interview the candidate over a period of an hour and form a judgment, or 'assess', whether he or she is competent to practice as a member of RICS. There are three main components to the interview: a critical analysis (submitted prior to interview); a presentation, during the interview, on that analysis; and a discussion with the assessors that targets the candidate's training and experience.

It is important to always bear in mind that the APC is primarily a period of training. Emphasis is placed on practical experience and it is this, rather than theoretical knowledge, that is tested in the final assessment interview.

WHO CAN TAKE THE APC?

Candidates who have graduated with an RICS-accredited degree and who have commenced employment or have relevant experience may take the APC. Part-time or distance learning undergraduates can start structured training in their final year, and part-time or distance learning postgraduates may do structured training concurrently.

There are a number of routes as set out previously, but this book concentrates on Graduate Routes 1 and 2 and does not cover Graduate Route 3, the Adaptation, Academic or Senior Professional routes to membership nor the route to 'technical membership' via the ATC (Assessment of Technical Competence). However, the guidance in this book on supporting, supervising and counselling candidates will be of help to anyone carrying out those roles for candidates on those routes. In addition, the information provided on the philosophies behind RICS membership will be invaluable to anyone seeking membership – through any route.

For more information on any of the other routes to membership, readers should contact the RICS Membership Operations Department or visit the RICS website, at www.rics.org.

WHO RUNS THE APC?

RICS is a membership organisation; decisions involving development or change are generally made by members sitting on various committees, on which RICS staff are also represented. The committee responsible for the APC in the UK is the UK Education and Standards Board. There are a number of such boards around the globe and their work is co-ordinated by the International Education Standards Board. These boards comprise groups of people representing the various national associations. Policy developments that affect the structure of the APC are subject to approval by the Education and Membership Committee, and any changes to the technical competencies by the appropriate RICS faculty board.

Each national association will normally be involved in one of the Education Standards Boards, which represents the broad spectrum of membership in the country or group of countries that form the association. The groups work with the International Board on issues and developments of mutual interest and concern.

For the last three years, representatives from the various boards have met at an international forum to discuss strategy and policy issues. The APC is thus extremely dynamic. It is constantly changing to meet the requirements of the modern business world and a strategy of international development and growth.

OFFICIAL GUIDANCE

Official guidance on the APC can be obtained from the RICS website, www.rics.org. In addition, there are two official guides available for candidates: the *APC/ATC requirements and competencies guide* and the *APC Candidate's Guide*.

A third guide exists for those guiding and supporting the candidates: the *APC Guide for supervisors, counsellors and employers*. This provides a basic introduction to the various roles, together with guidance on the duties and responsibilities of the parties.

These guides were revised in 2006 as a result of the changes that took place to the APC and an additional series of Pathway Guides were introduced to provide contextual guidance to the individual pathways from each faculty.

Further information on obtaining official guidance is provided in Chapter 9 of this book. It should be stressed that the advice in this book is not 'official' guidance. Should discrepancies arise between the advice provided in this book and the official APC guidance, the official material should always take precedence. In any case, supervisors and counsellors should carefully read all the official guidance available, and consult www.rics.org on a regular basis.

A last word of advice

Make sure you have a firm grasp of the basic requirements of the APC. The philosophies behind the APC are reflected in all aspects of the final assessment, and you must be well aware of all the key points to guide your candidate through the process successfully.

Getting the right candidates

2.

Before you can start supervising and counselling candidates through the APC, you must get hold of the candidates first. To attract the best candidates for your particular area of surveying, and geographical location, you must be able to offer them the best possible employment and APC package.

Recruitment of any new employee is an expensive business. Research shows costs of between £20,000–30,000 – expensive if you get it wrong. When trying to attract APC candidates, a good employer should start by considering whether all of the key ingredients are in place.

- Do you have a structured training agreement? (see Chapter 5 for more information on this) Most importantly, have you worked with an RICS training adviser (RTA) to have it 'approved'?

- What is your track record with previous graduates? Do you have pass rate percentages – and are they respectable enough to quote in job adverts?

- Do you have a lot of training modules and in-house programmes to support candidates on the APC, and for their career development generally?

- Is your firm IIP (Investors in People) or ISO (International Organization for Standardization) accredited? This indicates a commitment to employees.

- What is your plan to help candidates meet the requirements of the APC? Do you have a strategy of rotation to ensure that candidates will gain a range of skills?

- Do you have training programmes to support candidates in attaining the various competencies?

- Have you carried out any evaluation of your training scheme with your current graduates? If so, what have they told you about your performance?

- Do you have a training scheme for your APC supervisors and counsellors?

If you can answer 'yes' to all of the above questions, then you are ready to take on candidates. Being able to advertise the above will almost certainly help you to attract the best graduates, providing an instant return on your investment.

RECRUITMENT: A QUESTION OF 'FIT'

It is in everyone's interest to ensure that recruitment procedures select people that fit the organisation and job. The starting point in the recruitment of new staff is to consider what sort of person you are looking for, in the context of the culture of your organisation, your clients and customers, the team that the employee will be joining, and the skills required.

When advertising for employees, think carefully as to what information you can give about your organisation. The questions above show examples of the kind of things that attract the best APC candidates. You may also wish to offer visits to your office, so that candidates can experience the working environment first hand.

Application forms, interview techniques and assessments will all need careful consideration. Interviewing through the 'competence-based' approach discussed elsewhere in this book is a modern method, in which candidates are asked to give evidence of how they have employed their skills previously. This also fits neatly with the overall competence-based format of the APC, which I go on to discuss in later chapters.

Many large firms also hold 'assessment centre' selections to recruit graduate employees. In addition to a competence-based interview, other types of tests may be undertaken at these centres: aptitude tests, personality tests, group exercises and presentations.

A last word of advice

Recruitment and selection is a two-way process. To attract the best graduates and employees, you will need to impress them with a track record as one of the best trainers of APC candidates.

The role of the supervisor and counsellor

INTRODUCTION

When a candidate starts the APC process, he or she will be assigned a supervisor and counsellor from within his or her employer's firm. The supervisor and counsellor will be chosen by the employer, possibly in consultation with the human resources department. In some cases, candidates may suggest their own supervisor or counsellor, selecting someone they feel can act as a mentor and provide good support within their training area.

Supervisors and counsellors carry out a dual role: they advise and support the candidate throughout the process, and also assess the candidate's competence. They are not expected to train a candidate entirely by themselves, but rather, to make sure that the training the candidate receives during the course of carrying out his or her work in the firm matches and is applied to the requirements of the APC. They must organise and direct the training to ensure that this occurs, to avoid gaps in the candidate's experience. They should involve the candidate in all relevant work-based activities and encourage colleagues to do the same.

Supervisors and counsellors must also assist the candidate in complying with the requirements of the APC in terms of submitting material and filling out documentation, and must prepare them for the final assessment interview. Vitally, they are the people who 'sign off' the candidate as having passed the various stages and as being ready for the final assessment.

The supervisor should be the person who has day-to-day responsibility for the candidate and a good knowledge of his or her work. The counsellor has a more strategic role to play; he or she is responsible for planning the training programme and monitoring the progress of the candidate on an overall, 'big picture' basis, ensuring that it meets with the requirements of the candidate's chosen APC pathway.

The supervisor does not need to be RICS qualified, but the counsellor must be a chartered surveyor. Preferably, both should be members of RICS and should come from the same pathway that the candidate is following to membership. In practice, RICS will be comfortable with a non-chartered person carrying out the role of a supervisor, so long as they are suitably qualified to give guidance to the candidate concerning training and day-to-day work. Note also that it is acceptable for the counsellor to come from a different firm – a useful provision if there is no-one in the candidate's own firm able to fulfil that role.

There are significant differences between the roles of the supervisor and counsellor, and RICS would ideally wish the roles to be carried out by two different people. This allows the candidate access to two sets of knowledge, and should provide for a more impartial experience. However, in smaller firms, and under certain sets of circumstances, one person may be obliged to combine the two roles. If this happens, that person must be a member of RICS.

The roles are a heavy responsibility. In a moment we will consider the duties of both parties, in chronological order, from enrolment through to the final assessment –

and beyond. Before that, it may be useful to step back and consider the over-arching responsibilities for the entire training period.

In brief, as a supervisor or counsellor, you must:

- ensure, day to day, and week to week, that your candidate receives training in-line with the competency requirements of his or her chosen APC pathway;

- deliver coaching and training yourself, or ensure that the candidate receives training with someone else, for example, with another department in your firm;

- 'sign-off' the candidate at three-monthly and six-monthly intervals, and at the interim and final assessment stages;

- ensure that all records and reviews are completed accurately, reflect the requirements of the APC, and are submitted on time;

- assist the candidate with the preparation and submission of documents for the final assessment, and in preparation for the final assessment interview;

- liaise regularly with the supervisor/counsellor (if you are not the same person.); and

- provide support and encouragement, and generally be a good friend to the candidate, including on matters of general health and welfare.

The most important thing to realise is that your involvement with the training will be continuous, across the full training period – as will the process of assessment. You will not simply be 'dipping in and out' of the process.

WORKING TOGETHER

While not carrying out exactly the same roles, supervisors and counsellors should look to form an active partnership in terms of their respective responsibilities. This allows them to support one another, and provides a consistent management approach for the candidate. Under no circumstances should a situation arise in which the supervisor and counsellor are working against one another.

The active partnership should take the form of regular discussions and communications, outside of the formal six-monthly intervals, to head off any potential problems and ensure that the formal reviews run smoothly.

CHECKLIST OF ACTIONS

Having taken account of the over-arching responsibilities, we can now have a look at the nuts and bolts of the process, from the point of view of the supervisor and counsellor. Below, I provide brief notes on the duties to be performed, working through the process from 'Month 0' to the final assessment. You should treat this as a handy checklist – nothing more. The detail of the duties is discussed further in Chapter 4, when I examine each of these aspects more fully.

Bear in mind that the progression shown through the months below is that of 'an ideal world'. Business or other demands may prevent your candidate from completing the APC within the two years. Hopefully, though, this chronology, by clearly indicating the stages of the process, will allow you to view the procedures from start to finish – even if it is necessary to change the 'number' of the months in the headings.

The headings below relate to Graduate Route 1. Graduate Route 2 candidates will by-pass the reviews scheduled for months 9, 12, 15 and 18 in order to complete their training within the minimum 12 months.

Month 0: enrolment

Enrolment is the start of the APC process. The supervisor and counsellor must meet with the candidate and ensure that a satisfactory training and reviewing structure is in place, and must make sure all relevant documentation is returned promptly.

A delay of a few weeks of the candidate enrolling could put the final assessment back six months, as final assessments are normally held twice a year. Closing dates are given on www.rics.org.

Supervisor: actions

– Meet with the candidate and explain your role.

– Draw up a structured training agreement (or tailor your existing agreement to the particular candidate).

– Discuss and forward plan the candidate's training to ensure the competencies of the chosen pathway will be met to ensure that the achievement record will be satisfactorily completed.

– Check that the candidate returns all of the appropriate documentation to RICS in a prompt and timely fashion.

– Put dates in your diary for the three-, six- and 12-monthly reviews and make sure these are agreed between all parties required to attend.

Counsellor: actions

– Meet with the candidate and explain your role.

– Put dates in your diary for the six- and 12-monthly reviews and make sure that these are agreed between all parties.

Month 3: the three-monthly review

At the end of the first three months of training, the candidate and supervisor carry out a review. The supervisor's progress report (An example form can be found on www.rics.org) is completed, and the training process reviewed.

Supervisor: actions

– Check that the candidate has got off to a good start with the training period and is progressing as planned: review the training agreement and progress against the various competencies of the chosen pathway.

– Sign off any competency levels that have been reached, in the achievement record (Templates 4 and 5).

– Review the professional development record (Template 3), to ensure the candidate is making good progress in this area.

– Check the candidate is filling in the diary (example form on www.rics.org) and log book (Template 2) as required.

– Complete the Supervisor's progress report (example form on www.rics.org).

Counsellor: actions

– Although you have no formal role to play at this stage, for reasons of good management it is desirable for you to speak to the supervisor, to ensure that everything is on track. That way, if problems have arisen, or are likely to arise, efforts can be made to head them off early, rather than waiting for the more formal review process – by which point minor issues may have become major difficulties.

Month 6: the six-monthly review

At the end of six months there is a further review, in which the counsellor is involved. The aim is similar to that of the three-monthly review: to ensure that the candidate is progressing well against the competencies and that documentation is up-to-date. The Counsellor's progress report is to be completed here, while the supervisor will also complete another report – example forms for both may be found on www.rics.org

Supervisor: actions

–   Check that the candidate is progressing with the training as planned: review the training agreement and progress against the various competencies of the chosen pathway.

–   Sign off any competency levels that have been reached, in the achievement record.

–   Review the professional development record, to ensure the candidate is making good progress.

–   Check the candidate is filling in the diary and log book as required.

–   Complete the Supervisor's progress report (example form on www.rics.org).

Counsellor: actions

–   Review the candidate's training and achievements to date.

–   Assess the candidate's performance against the competencies, signing off any if appropriate in the achievement record (Templates 4 and 5).

–   Complete the Counsellor's progress report (example form on www.rics.org).

Month 9: another three-monthly review

The supervisor will carry out another three-monthly review.

Supervisor: actions

–   Check that the candidate is progressing with the training as planned: review the training agreement and progress against the competencies

- Sign off any competency levels that have been reached, in the achievement record.
- Review the professional development record, to check on the candidate's progress.
- Check the candidate is filling in the diary and log book as required.
- Complete the Supervisor's progress report (example form on www.rics.org).

Counsellor: actions

- You have no formal role to play at this point, but again, it is a good idea to liaise with the supervisor, to gain an idea of overall progress.

Month 12: the interim assessment

Within one month of recording 12 months of training, or on the completion of a sandwich placement from the date of enrolment, an interim assessment of the training and experience the candidate has gained up to that date is held. Both the supervisor and counsellor are involved in this. The discussion should be lengthier and more in-depth than for the preceding reviews, with three forms to be completed: The interim assessment record (template 6), the counsellor and supervisor progress reports and a declaration of completion of the interim assessment record (to be sent to RICS, see template 7).

These completed forms will need to be sent to RICS within one month of recording 12 months of training. Failure to submit the forms completed correctly will delay the date of your candidate's final assessment.

Supervisor: actions

- Review the progress of your candidate to date: consider the level of competencies reached and the professional development that has been undertaken.

- Sign off any competency levels that have been reached, in the achievement record (Templates 4 and 5).

- Review the professional development record (Template 3).

- Check the candidate is filling in the diary and log book as required.

- With the candidate, plan the final 12 months of training.

- With the candidate and counsellor, complete Templates 6 and 7 (see Chapter 4 for more information on this).

- The counsellor and supervisor will also need to complete reports (example forms on www.rics.org)

- Encourage the candidate to begin considering the critical analysis.

Counsellor: actions

- Review the candidate's training and achievements to date.

- Assess the candidate's performance against the competencies and sign off any competency levels that have been reached, in the achievement record (Templates 4 and 5).

- Review the professional development record (Template 3).

- With the candidate and supervisor, complete Templates 6 and 7.

- Encourage the candidate to begin considering the critical analysis.

Month 15: another three-monthly review

The supervisor will carry out another three-monthly review at this point.

Supervisor: actions

– Check that the candidate is progressing with the training as planned.

– Sign off any competency levels that have been reached, in the achievement record (Templates 4 and 5).

– Review the candidate's professional development record, to check on progress in this area (Template 3).

– Check the candidate is filling in the diary and log book as required.

– Complete another Supervisor's progress report (example form on www.rics.org).

– Check that the candidate is ready to start work on the critical analysis.

Counsellor: actions

– Again, you have no formal role to play at this point, but should take the opportunity to liaise with the supervisor over the candidate's progress. As the time for the final assessment approaches, it is increasingly important that all parties are aware of what progress has been made, and what is left to achieve.

Month 18: another six-monthly review

There is now a further six-monthly review, involving both the supervisor and counsellor. The aim, as before, is to ensure that the candidate is progressing well against the competencies, and that documentation is up-to-date.

Supervisor: actions

– Check that the candidate is progressing with the training as planned.

- Sign off any competency levels that have been reached in the achievement record (Templates 4 and 5).

- Review the professional development record (Template 3).

- Check the candidate is filling in the diary and log book as required.

- Check that work on the critical analysis is underway.

- Complete another Supervisor's progress report (example form on www.rics.org).

- Start thinking about how best to prepare the candidate for the final assessment interview. If any mock interviews are to be arranged, this is the point at which to do so.

Counsellor: actions

- Review the candidate's training and achievements to date.

- Assess the candidate's performance against the competencies; sign off any that have been attained in the achievement record (Templates 4 and 5).

- Check that work on the critical analysis is underway.

- Complete another Counsellor's progress report (example form on www.rics.org).

- Start thinking about how best to prepare the candidate for the final assessment interview. If any mock interviews are to be arranged, this is the point at which to do so.

Month 21 (Month 9 for Graduate Route 2) – another three-monthly review

At this point as well as the normal actions taken for a three-month review, particular attention should be paid to preparation for the final assessment.

At the end of minimum 23 months (minimum 11 months for Graduate Route 2)

This is the earliest point at which the candidate is signed off by the supervisor and counsellor as being ready for the final assessment.

The supervisor and counsellor will ensure that the candidate submits the necessary documentation to RICS, ready for the final assessment. You will have decided the target final assessment date with the candidate at the beginning of their training. The candidate will receive a letter from RICS confirming the assessment centre, date and time normally four weeks before the assessment date.

Supervisor: actions

– Sign off any competency levels that have been reached, in the achievement record (Templates 4 and 5).

– Review the professional development record to ensure that a satisfactory number of hours have been achieved over a range of activities (Template 3).

– Ensure the log book is up-to-date and has the correct number of days logged (Template 2).

– Check the critical analysis is complete, has been signed and forwarded to RICS.

– Making use of all previous records and reviews, ensure the candidate fills in Template 8, the final assessment record.

– Ensure the candidate submits the necessary documentation to RICS on time (a list of this is provided in Chapter 4). Thoroughly check that this documentation is complete and accurate and an incomplete submission will be returned by RICS and final assessment will be delayed by six months.

– Offer advice to the candidate on the final assessment interview.

Counsellor: actions

– Sign off any competency levels that have been reached, in the achievement record.

– Double-check the professional development record (Template 3) to ensure that a satisfactory number of hours has been achieved.

– Double-check that the log book (Template 2) is up-to-date.

– Offer advice to the candidate on the final assessment interview.

A last word of advice

Supervisors and counsellors must work together. Your candidate needs a coherent management approach, in order to progress with confidence.

In Chapter 4, we discuss all of these stages in detail. The documentation referred to is discussed further in Chapter 5.

In detail: supervisor and counsellor duties

In the previous chapter, I discussed the roles of the supervisor and counsellor in brief, giving checklists for use throughout the training period. This chapter aims to 'flesh out' those checklists and notes, to give you a fuller understanding of what is required from you in your roles. Once again, I adopt a chronological approach, following the Graduate Route 1 candidate from enrolment, through to the final assessment – and beyond. For Graduate Route 2 candidates the time taken to complete the process will be halved.

At each of the stages noted below, I mention the need to follow the competencies set out in the APC guides. It is essential that supervisors and counsellors have a firm grasp of what exactly the competencies are – and of how they should be measured and assessed. The competencies are discussed – and explained – in detail in Chapters 6 and 7.

Although the roles can be divided up into stages, the APC is a process of continuous training and assessment – the supervisor (and to a lesser degree, the counsellor) does not simply dip in and out of the training at certain specified dates. Your involvement with the candidate's progress is continuous, and your assessment and training plan must be continuous and progressive also. It may therefore be helpful to start with a quick look at the nature of the assessment process overall.

CONTINUOUS, PROGRESSIVE, COMPETENCE-BASED ASSESSMENT

Continuous assessment

The APC process is one of continual training and learning. It is therefore one of continuous assessment too. Although the final assessment will be carried out by trained APC assessors, supervisors and counsellors are involved in the ongoing assessment of candidates over the full course of the two-year training period. You are called upon to make formal judgments on the competence of candidates at certain specific stages, to certify that they meet the standards set by RICS.

If you are the candidate's supervisor, it is likely that you will already be doing much of what is required to assess him or her, as this requires similar processes to those used for appraising staff. Assessment involves being aware of how the candidate is performing in day-to-day activities and looking at work he or she has produced. From this, you can begin to form a judgment of how well he or she is doing.

If your candidate is in another department, or on secondment, you will have to work a little harder. By observing your candidate at work in that department, you will be able to assess some of the requirements of the mandatory competencies, such as working in a team, problem-solving and working to deadlines. By looking at work the candidate has produced, you will be able to learn more about his or her technical and professional knowledge, as well as his or her understanding.

Obviously, you should keep notes and records of how your candidate is doing, to help you with the 'signing off' of the competencies. Keep such notes regularly, not just when a formal review is approaching, to give you a thorough overview of his or her performance.

Progressive assessment

One of the basic philosophies of the APC is the idea that candidates will learn skills and acquire experience progressively. This is embodied in the levels set out for the various competencies, in which candidates are expected to progress from a 'knowledge and understanding' of a particular area, through to practical experience of that area under normal circumstances, and finally, to gain the ability to apply their knowledge in more complex circumstances, and to evaluate a situation in a wider context.

The competencies are drawn up with three levels to reflect this progressive approach. I consider this in some detail in Chapter 6 – meanwhile, supervisors and counsellors should bear in mind, as noted throughout this chapter, that the candidate's records must show a progressive approach to learning. Supervisors and counsellors do not wait until a candidate has reached Level 3 before 'signing them off' – but rather indicate how they have progressed through Levels 1 and 2, in earlier records and reviews, to reach this higher level. The final assessment panel will take a dim view of all competencies being signed off on the same day, in the same colour pen; it implies that the progressive approach has not been adopted – or at least, not properly monitored.

In the APC, the process is as important as the end point.

Competence-based assessment

The APC consists of competence-based assessment. This is assessment of actual performance, or competence, at work. It seeks to ascertain that the candidate not only has the necessary knowledge and understanding to carry out his or her work, but can also put this knowledge into practice. Traditional qualifications tend to test what people know, whereas the competence-based approach, while still assessing what they know, also assesses what they can do.

In fact, the APC and, in particular, the final assessment interview can be thought of as adopting a part competence-based approach. In the main, as described above, this is a test of actual experience. However, at certain points in the final assessment interview, the assessors will 'step outside' of the candidate's experience, and ask him or her wider questions on a particular issue. This type of questioning is discussed in more detail on page 49.

Your assessment and reviews should prepare the candidate for this type of approach. First, ask your candidate to provide you with examples of practical occasions on which they have put their knowledge into practice. Ask them to explain what approach they adopted in a particular instance, and to analyse the effectiveness of that. Then, try to extend this experience, asking them about factors surrounding the actual experience – potential problems that could arise another time, for example. Again, see page 49 for more information on this type of questioning.

I will now look at the roles of the supervisor and counsellor in more detail, starting at the very beginning of the APC process.

ENROLMENT

Enrolment is the start of your APC candidate's journey to membership. It will also form an important part of your candidate's first impressions of you (as supervisor or counsellor), and your firm.

I would suggest that supervisors and counsellors hold a short meeting to brief their candidates on the APC process, and to provide an overview of what it entails. They should stress the importance of completing the enrolment forms as soon as possible. The sooner your candidate is enrolled by RICS, the sooner the candidate will be able to start adding days of training – and the sooner he or she will be able to consider the final assessment. More information on these documents is given in Chapter 5.

The supervisor and counsellor must also discuss and agree the competencies to be achieved, considering the candidate's chosen pathway to membership, and the resources of the firm. (The competencies, and how to choose them, are discussed in detail in Chapters 6 and 7.) This is also the point to discuss how the training will be complemented by professional development.

Overall, it is important to give the candidate an insight into how you intend managing the partnership over the two years that will follow. Discuss and agree expectations – your own, and your candidate's. Make sure that all sides start with a clear vision and understanding of the events that will follow.

End the process by putting dates in your diaries for the three-, six-and 12-monthly reviews, and make sure that these are agreed by all the parties required to attend. This ensures a pro-active approach to managing the candidate's training, creates a good impression, and should ensure that the dates do not slip.

THREE-MONTHLY REVIEWS

The objective of the first three-monthly review is to allow the supervisor to verify that the candidate has got off to a good start with the training period. A lot of your views and opinions concerning the candidate's progress will come from your observations, discussions and contact with the candidate during the early part of the training period. This is, in effect, continuous assessment in action.

Care is needed at this early stage. All candidates develop at different rates, and their speed of development may vary from competency to competency. Sometimes candidates will make a slow start until they grasp or become familiar with basic concepts, but may then 'take off', with a rapid rate of development. The reverse may also apply, with candidates quick to pick up on initial points, but slower to transfer these into practice. Other candidates will follow a more consistent or 'straight line' rate of development. Remember to respect the diversity of approach – we are all different.

I remember a supervisor mentioning to me that she had concerns about a candidate who appeared to be progressing slowly in the initial stages, particularly in the core and optional competencies of the pathway. The candidate was a particularly thorough young man, who wished to be very sure of his ground, and would double- and triple-check the requirements for each situation. I heard again from the supervisor a month or two later. She had been surprised by what occurred shortly after speaking to me. The candidate, having absorbed all the necessary information and processes, had begun to progress faster than her other candidates in almost all areas.

In another instance, a supervisor was very impressed by a candidate who initially gained a lot of ground, picking up the easier concepts very quickly. Expecting this rate of development to continue uninterruptedly, the candidate was given more responsibility than was usual, for a fairly large and complex project. Unfortunately, it seemed that this was a case of 'too much, too soon' – the candidate soon got into difficulties, which to his credit he immediately revealed to his managers. The project was saved – but the candidate's confidence a little dented. Always make sure you keep a careful eye on the pace of development.

The three-monthly reviews are also the point at which the supervisor concentrates on the candidate's management of the various APC documents. For the first three-monthly review, you will need to consider the following documents:

- the candidate's diary;
- the candidate's log book and professional development record; and
- the achievement record.

Chapter 5 provides details of each of these documents. Ensure that the candidate is filling them in, or following them, as necessary.

Prior to the first review, get hold of a copy of the *APC candidate's guide* and the *APC/ATC requirements and competencies guide*, in addition to any notes or examples of work to which you want to refer. Set aside a time and a place where you will be undisturbed for an hour or so. These reviews are very personal, so if you work in a large, open-plan office, book a room where you will have some quiet and privacy.

A useful starting point in any review (or appraisal) is to ask the candidate to prepare a few notes in readiness for the meeting – this will help to focus the candidate's mind, and will allow you to open the meeting by asking how he or she feels the training is going and what progress has been made. I normally find that when approached in this way, the majority of people are very honest in their views and opinions.

Your discussion in the review will need to relate specifically to progress against the competencies. Ask the candidate to bring some examples of his or her work, to support his or her view of the level of attainment he or she has reached in the various competencies. Try to 'stretch' the candidate's knowledge and experience. Ask what he or she has learned from a particular situation, what problems were faced, and how they were resolved, and how the experience could be transferred or adapted to deal with other areas of work. This ability to learn, and then transfer skills and experience to address other problems, will form an important aspect of the final assessment interview, particularly for those competencies which are required to Level 3. It also allows you to check that the candidate has a good all-round view of any particular situation or technique, enabling them to repeat their actions under different circumstances.

At the end of each three-monthly review, you will be able to complete the Supervisor's progress report (an example form can be found on www.rics.org). This asks you to make some notes concerning 'training to date, experience gained and ability of the candidate'. I would suggest that at the first three-month stage, your views concerning the ability of the candidate will be very general; however, you should keep an accurate record of your discussions around the competencies. Later reviews will be able to draw upon more information. The candidate will also need to add some comments to the progress report – these need only be brief. The notes on the report will also be useful for the counsellor, who will be involved in the six-monthly meeting and will need to review evidence of progress.

After filling in the form, it must be signed and dated by you and the candidate. Don't forget that when you do this, it is your professional integrity and reputation you are committing to paper. Treat this report with the same degree of diligence and professionalism as you would any other report going out of the office with your signature on it.

Example templates are available on www.rics.org or two different examples of three-monthly progress reports are shown on pages 31–35.

At this stage, supervisors may also be able to sign off some of the competencies in the candidate's achievement record (Templates 4 and 5). If you do plan to sign off a competency, check that the candidate feels confident at the level being discussed before you do so.

Try to include a few 'action points' in the progress record as well, as this will signal to the candidate that he or she has an active partnership with you. Be realistic about what can be signed-off after the first three months – you may be able to sign off perhaps one or two Level 1 technical competencies in the core and optional areas and one or two mandatory competencies to Level 1.

At this stage you should also check the candidate's professional development record (Template 3) to make sure that good progress is being made in this area. You would expect to see around 12 hours recorded here, although it could be more, if the candidate has undergone a lot of induction training in the first few months.

Note that the process carried out in the first three-monthly review must be repeated for subsequent reviews. For the later reviews, you will have much more information about the candidate and will be able to hold more focused discussions.

SAMPLE SUPERVISOR'S PROGRESS REPORT A

To be completed every three months.

(Note: This form is for the use of candidates and supervisors. It is not to be submitted to RICS.)

Date: 7th April 2007 (Period January 2007 to March 2007) – Observations on training to date, experience gained and ability of candidate:

Training to date

Laura has attended a two-day 'managing relationships at work' course. This course has added to her already developed ability to get on well with a variety of work colleagues and to appreciate their styles of approach.

Laura has built up a solid base in her first three months. In particular she has been able to produce financial appraisals and liaise with sub-consultants on such matters with the minimum of supervision.

- Report writing – soft market testing report, cash flow report

- Cash flow calculations – cash flow appraisal

- Brochure wording and questionnaire

- Evaluation process

- Market testing exercise with lead developers

- Involvement on report editing

Research – Laura has researched market evidence for residential space in connection with regeneration projects.

Client contact – Client exposure has increased dramatically and Laura has handled clients well.

Ability of Candidate

Interpersonal skills – Laura is a good team member and fits in well. She has a good rapport with clients.

Written material – Laura has an appropriate use of business English and presents information in an organised manner.

Numerical – Laura has an excellent understanding of figures and the ability to use relevant systems and create cashflow spreadsheets.

Self-management – Laura makes good use of the working day to earn fees and has absorbed quickly the fundamentals of drafting and issuing invoices.

Signature: N Bursar Date: 7 April 2007

Candidate's comments:

During my first three months within the Public Sector Consultancy team, I have worked on a number of interesting, large-scale local authority development schemes. The majority of the work carried out has been in the form of development appraisal analysis and other numerical tasks. I am thoroughly enjoying my work within the team and am continually learning from the other members of the team.

I feel a valued member of the department and believe that I have shown many of my strengths in the work that I have undertaken. During the next three months I hope to gain more experience in some of the areas in which I am not so competent, such as letter writing and report drafting. Also, during this period I would like to gain experience in general areas of surveying, such as landlord and tenant issues.

Signature: Laura Marshall Date: 7 April 2007

SAMPLE SUPERVISOR'S PROGRESS REPORTS B

To be completed every three months.

(Note: This form is for the use of candidates and supervisors. It is not to be submitted to RICS.)

Date: 6 February 2007 – Observations on training to date, experience gained and ability of candidate:

Initially, Richard was given an overview of the firm and its organisation. This was followed by a review of the records kept (both paper and computer-based) and where to find them. The firm's intranet was also demonstrated, and details of where to find data relevant to Richard's day-to-day work provided.

Richard has attended a residential course, which covers the requirements of RICS guidance, legal aspects of his work and current environmental issues.

With regard to practical experience, Richard has so far mainly concentrated on residential property, although some commercial property has been covered. He has carried out valuations for inheritance and capital gains tax purposes, and is familiar with market value, the valuation of undivided shares and matters such as special purchasers and goodwill. He has encountered regulated, assured shorthold tenancies, and appreciates their impact on value.

Richard has also been introduced to the inspection of buildings. He has been able to assemble comparable evidence, analyse it and apply the results to valuations. He has carried out reports for Housing Associations, and has negotiated values with solicitors and surveyors.

Richard has responded extremely well to the challenges he has faced, and is enthusiastic and keen to learn. He has worked hard and made good progress.

Signature: P Goody Date: 6 February 2007

Candidate's comments:

I have learned a great deal in the short time I have been employed at the firm. Initially I was introduced to the bases of inheritance tax and capitals gains tax, and progressed from carrying out initial appraisals to inspecting and valuing residential properties under supervision.

The cases with which I have been involved so far have raised many issues in respect of statute and case law, which I am reviewing on a regular basis. I have begun to negotiate with agents, which has ensured that I am thorough with my valuations and has enhanced my oral communication skills.

In the next three months, I hope to gain experience in valuing commercial properties, which I hope will raise additional landlord and tenant issues that will further my competence in this area.

I have gained much from my first three months at the firm, and have enjoyed being part of such a friendly and supportive team.

Signature: Richard Fitzwilliam Date: 6 February 2007

SIX-MONTHLY REVIEWS

As far as the supervisor is concerned, the process for the six-monthly reviews will be very similar to that for the three-monthly reviews. You should carry out the actions noted above, and fill in another report on the appropriate template. The main difference at this juncture is the involvement of the counsellor. The counsellor is involved to assess the candidate against the competencies, to review overall progress, to provide a second opinion to that of the supervisor, and in so doing, to complete the Counsellor's progress report. The idea is that the counsellor will take a strategic overview, to ensure that everything is on track. The counsellor should question progress, assist with areas of uncertainty, and most importantly, add an additional viewpoint to proceedings. This makes it clear why RICS prefers the two roles to be carried out by two separate people.

The counsellor should review the documentation, with a view to checking the number of days of training undertaken – it should be around 100 at the first six-monthly review, noted in the log book – and to check that progress is being made against the various competencies and levels. Do remember that the overriding approach, at the first six-monthly review, should be one that is progressive and reasonable for a candidate who is approaching the quarter-way mark: perhaps signed off to Levels 1 or 2 in a number of competencies, with probably around three or four mandatory competencies completed. There should be a reasonable spread of days allocated to each competency in the log book.

In addition, check the number of hours recorded for professional development. At the first six-month stage, you would expect to see around 24 hours noted in Template 3.

Having checked the documentation, the next step is to discuss the candidate's progress with the supervisor. There may be issues that require clarification, or over which you have concerns, or you may detect problems. After discussions with the supervisor, and if you feel that everything is on track, you should then speak to the candidate together with the supervisor. (If a joint meeting is difficult for reasons of distance, consider holding a telephone conference.)

If you have concerns and require a separate discussion with the candidate, then let the supervisor know that you are doing this. Make it clear that it is with the best intentions of both parties in mind and with the ultimate goal of ensuring that the candidate successfully completes the APC. After talking to the candidate, complete the loop by holding a further discussion with the supervisor, which may be merely to say that you are now happy, or perhaps to suggest some corrective action.

The precise approach adopted by the counsellor is likely to reflect the degree of contact the counsellor has with the candidate and supervisor. This may be regular and structured where all parties are working in the same office or in close geographical proximity, or much less frequent if the role is being carried out from a distance. In the latter case, a more formal approach to the six-monthly reviews may be required.

The counsellor should ensure that all actions and discussions are documented on the appropriate Template. You should state whether you and the supervisor had a joint meeting with the candidate or whether this was carried out separately. If you have adopted a tri-party approach, the completion of your report may be a repeat of the supervisor's report.

An example of a completed progress report is provided below.

A further six-monthly review is held at month 18. This process should be repeated then, with more information being available to you about the candidate as the training period progresses.

SAMPLE COUNSELLOR'S PROGRESS REPORTS

To be completed every six months. (Please do not complete this section if you are also the candidate's supervisor)

(Note: This form is for the use of candidates and counsellors. It is not to be submitted to RICS.)

Date: 30 June 2007

Comments and recommendations:

On 29 June I held a joint meeting with the candidate and supervisor to discuss Richard's progress.

Richard has made an excellent start.

He has quickly become proficient at domestic valuations for national taxation purposes and has very capably dealt with residential valuations for other purposes. His valuations and reports are clear, well-considered and show a good understanding of the legal and valuation background.

He is a natural negotiator and is increasing in experience.

Richard is well-organised, conscientious, reliable, a quick learner and is already an invaluable and well-liked member of the team.

Over the final months with our team, we will arrange the compulsory purchase order experience that he now needs. I have changed Richard's work allocation, so that he will deal with a core West End location, in order to increase his commercial valuation experience.

Signature: A Sedley Date: 30 June 2007

Candidate's comments:

In the last three months I have been given a greater variety of work, ranging from residential and commercial valuations, to the valuation of goodwill, compulsory purchase and compensation cases.

I carry out the majority of my inspections alone, although I discuss many of the issues that arise with my supervisor, to benefit from his experience.

In the next six months, I hope to improve my working knowledge of building construction and to gain further experience in compulsory purchase work and landlord and tenant issues, in order to attain the required competencies.

Signature: Richard Fitzwilliam Date: 30 June 2007

12-MONTH INTERIM ASSESSMENT

The date of the interim assessment is important; a minimum of a further 12 months of training must be completed after this date, before the candidate can apply for the final assessment. The assessment should take place within one month of completing the 12 months.

For the supervisor, this is a very significant juncture in the APC. It gives you the opportunity to sit down with your candidate to review progress and to plan the final 12 months of training. The counsellor also meets with the candidate again at this stage.

There are two forms that need to be completed:

- the interim assessment record (Template 6); and

- a copy of the declaration of completion of interim assessment (Template 7).

It should be noted that this last document was introduced as part of the review of the APC in 2006 and should be submitted within one month of completion of the first 12 months structured training – failure to do so could result in a delay to the final assessment date.

The 12-month review should take a similar format to that described for the three- and six-monthly reviews above. However, as this is such an important point in the candidate's training period more time should be devoted to the meeting. In preparation the candidate should be asked to complete Template 6 (Interim assessment record) using notes from previous reviews and entries in the achievement record to help.

This Template should be reviewed by the supervisor and counsellor, with a discussion based around any 'gaps' in experience that are revealed. Any such gaps will form the basis of the candidate's training needs over the next 12 months.

The supervisor and counsellor should then complete their observations in the 'future training' section of the template and then sign the document.

The template is sent to RICS by the candidate as one of the submission documents shortly before the final assessment interview, and will be considered by the panel of assessors as an important component of the final assessment.

As part of the interim assessment, and to assist in filling in the above templates, the supervisor and counsellor should ensure that the candidate's log book has been completed and is in line with the training plan. The log book should show a good balance in terms of the number of entries across the spread of competencies, and should start to show that the candidate is on the way to fulfilling the requirements of his or her chosen APC pathway.

You are also likely to be able to sign off some more competencies in Templates 4 and 5. Remember that this process should be progressive. There should be a reasonable number of days attributed to each competency. At this stage, you should also hope to see around 48 hours of professional development noted in Template 3, linked to the candidate's training plan, and balanced fairly equally across the range of skills. Again, it will be the gaps in these templates that will indicate exactly what is left to be achieved in the next 12 months.

Template 6: Interim Assessment Record

This form requires the candidate to write, in approximately 2,000 words, an account of the first 12 months' training and experience. There is also a section in which to note training planned for the second part of the training period. This may comprise a note of competencies or levels where further experience is needed.

It is recommended that the candidate writes 500 words under the mandatory competencies headings, 1000 words in respect of the technical competencies and finally 500 words in respect of professional development (PD). The candidate needs to give a broad indication of the dates when training and experience has been completed. This may be simply 'in the first six months', 'in months two to ten' or, for competencies such as ethics, professional identity and accountability, 'over the full 12-month period'.

The candidate should then give some details of the experience or training undertaken. Particularly with regard to the core and optional competencies, the candidate may use his or her diary to give some specific examples of the work done, indicating its particular nature and any problems encountered during attainment of the various levels of competency. This kind of information is very useful to the final assessment panel and will help them with their approach to questions, ensuring that these relate to the candidate's actual experience.

Under the 'mandatory competencies' heading, the candidate should outline in a few sentences how the level in each competency has been reached: through structured reading, a CPD event, a training course, or in conjunction with undertaking training and experience around some of the core and optional competencies.

The space to note information about professional development should include a history of the main elements of PD so far undertaken, with a summary of the key learning gained. At all times, supervisors and counsellors should look for clearly defined links between the candidate's professional development and the competencies. There must be evidence of a planned and systematic approach, as opposed to an ad hoc or random selection of professional development topics. If the candidate is training to be a valuation surveyor, a two-hour lecture on rocket science would not be an appropriate choice of professional development.

The final section of this form is for training planned. This should comprise a brief note of what the supervisor and counsellor feel is required.

Supervisors and counsellors should ask the candidate to prepare Template 6 in a draft format, to be discussed and finalised at the interim assessment meeting.

SAMPLE TEMPLATE 6

(Graduate Route 1 only)

Months 1–12

Please record your summary of experience/training completed with reference to specific competencies where applicable.

This must be sent to RICS with your final assessment submissions

NB: Maximum 2,000 words

	Summary of experience/training completed
Mandatory 500 words	
Technical 1,000 words	
PD 500 words	

Future training (written by the supervisor and counsellor)

Supervisor's Signature: Date:

Name:(CAPITALS)   **Mem. No.:**

Counsellor's Signature: Date:

Name:(CAPITALS)   **Mem. No.:**

It should be noted as a result of the 2006 review of the APC this form is a replacement for two previous forms and combines progress with a forward plan/future training which should be written by the supervisor counsellor. When completing your part of this form it is important that you are as specific as possible concerning both the nature of the events planned and the timing of events.

A note on the critical analysis

It might be worth discussing with your candidate at this point the choice of project(s) for the critical analysis (a written report of a maximum of 3,000 words, comprising a detailed analysis of a project, or projects, with which the candidate has been extensively involved during the training period). There are now only around nine months before the candidate needs to start writing the critical analysis, and it is well worth starting to plan ahead. The candidate may wish to choose a topic that has already been covered in the first 12 months of training, or perhaps to identify a potential area of work or project that is coming on stream in the first six months of the second 12 months of training.

The choice of topic for the critical analysis is very important. Guidance is given on this in the *APC candidate's guide* and in the RICS Books guide, *APC 2006 – your practical guide to success*. It is important to remember that the subject (or subjects) chosen do not have to be anything exciting or unusual. It is perfectly acceptable for a candidate to submit an analysis dealing with his or her role in the valuation of an ordinary small shop for a rent review (for example) – so long as it is a project in which he or she was extensively involved, and fulfils all the other requirements for the analysis, as discussed on page 69. Too many candidates seem to feel that the only suitable choice of subject is something akin to the construction of a multi-million-pound dam in the desert. Having said that, if your candidate has been involved in such a venture, he or she is free to write about that.

Candidates should ensure that the subject(s) chosen will provide them with plenty of 'meat' for the analysis and their presentation on this. They should choose subjects they can 'get an angle on' – something on which they perhaps encountered difficulties, with a note on how these were overcome. Showy projects may look superficially impressive, but if the candidate has not been thoroughly involved, he or she will not be able to write or talk impressively on the subject. All in all, make sure your candidate gives him or herself the best possible chance to demonstrate competence.

A final point

There is one final, important point to note with regard to interim assessments. RICS training advisers (RTAs) may ask to see interim assessment documentation whilst carrying out routine visits to employers. Failure to provide such evidence will result in the candidate's final assessment being delayed.

ACTIONS AT 18 MONTHS

At 18 months, with another six-monthly review underway, the most important point is to make sure your candidate has begun work on the critical analysis. The critical analysis is covered in more detail in Chapter 5.

At this stage, you would expect your candidate to be about two-thirds to three-quarters of the way through the APC process, having completed about 300 days of training. He or she will probably be at about Level 2 for most competencies, with some perhaps attained to Level 3. The candidate may well have completed about 72 hours of professional development.

ACTIONS AT 21 MONTHS

This is a critical three-monthly review. Apart from carrying out the normal actions, you will need to make sure your candidate applies for the final assessment. It is also important to check your candidate's progress towards completion of the critical analysis and also to ensure that all other documentation is on course. Your candidate needs to be ready both in terms of paperwork and personal preparation for the final assessment, which will take place at some point over the next three to four months (deadline dates are available on www.rics.org and are different for each faculty.

This may also be a useful juncture to start planning more detailed actions to prepare your candidate for the final assessment, such as presentation skills training and arranging any mock interviews.

ACTIONS AT 23/24 MONTHS

At 23 months, your candidate is only about one to two months from the final assessment interview. If all is going well, and to plan, this is the point at which the supervisor and counsellor will 'sign off' the candidate for the assessment.

The way the run up to final assessment works is that the candidate, in conjunction with the supervisor, will have already chosen one of the dates for final assessment – the final assessment information is on www.rics.org. Supervisors and counsellors will need to ensure that the completed application forms have been submitted within the dates specified on www.rics.org. There will then follow a period of approximately one month to complete and send to RICS the required documents for the final assessment presentation and interview.

Supervisors and counsellors must also ensure at this point that the candidate submits the correct documentation to RICS and that this is up-to-date with all competencies completed. If the documentation is incorrect or incomplete RICS will return it and the candidate's final assessment date will be delayed by six months.

To ascertain your candidate's readiness for the final assessment and to make sure everything is ready to be submitted to RICS, you should review all documentation, to check that it is up-to-date and correctly filled in:

- Make sure the diary is up-to-date.

- Ensure the log book makes sense in terms of the number of days noted in total and the spread of training against each of the competencies.

- Ensure that all competencies have been reached and have been signed off in the achievement record.

- Check the professional development record shows the appropriate number of hours of learning. For a candidate sitting the final assessment after two-year's training and experience it should note a minimum of

96 hours of professional development, with a balanced reflection of the requirements of the core, optional and mandatory competencies, and professional practice skills.

- Make sure the critical analysis has been completed.
- Check that the templates that make up the interim assessment are complete.

The candidate must then submit the following:

- marksheets;
- professional education and employment record;
- the log book (Template 2);
- the record of professional development (Template 3);
- the achievement record (including Templates 4 and 5);
- the interim assessment record (Template 6);
- the final assessment record (Template 8)
- the critical analysis; and
- a copy of the candidate's certificate of accredited qualification

Once these submissions are received by RICS, the candidate will be sent confirmation of the date, time and venue of the final assessment (this will be one month prior to the assessment).

If, having reviewed this documentation, it is clear that the candidate will not be ready for the final assessment date notified by RICS, then this must be deferred. Entering an under-prepared candidate for final assessment will result in referral. It is a waste of everyone's time (and your money) to send a candidate with days of training incomplete, or a professional development record short on hours, and have them immediately referred.

To defer the date of the assessment, you should contact RICS immediately. The onus is on the candidate to notify RICS that they wish to defer.

The responsibility therefore lies with the supervisor and counsellor to ensure that the candidate is competent in all of the required areas before applying for the final assessment. In essence, when you certify that the candidate is ready to sit his or her APC, it is your professional judgment that you are putting on the line. It should be remembered that 400 days/24 calendar months for a Graduate Route 1 candidate or 200 days/12 calendar months for a Graduate Route 2 Candidate is a minimum training period. It is vital that candidates are not sent for final assessment too early. Failure (a referral) is not only disappointing for them, but very time-consuming for everyone involved, including the supervisor and counsellor.

However, if you have carried out the actions noted in the rest of this book properly, then your candidate should be ready, and all of this documentation should be up-to-date.

The assessment panel will receive all of the above documentation about four weeks before the final assessment interview. Remember, this will be their first impression of your candidate (and, incidentally, of you). Make sure it is a good one! It is important that the documentation is complete, well-presented, signed and dated.

I would add one last word of warning at this stage. Month 24 and the final assessment will soon approach, and may be followed very quickly by the final assessment interview. If you are planning to organise mock interviews (or similar) for your candidate, or to set aside a time to provide advice on the final assessment, you will need to plan these actions well in advance. It may be around the 20 or 21 month reviews that you start planning any such activities.

PREPARATION FOR THE FINAL ASSESSMENT INTERVIEW

While you will play an important part in preparing the candidate for the final assessment interview, ultimately they will be on their own in the interview room. You should therefore encourage them to prepare themselves as much as possible. The RICS Books publication, *APC 2006 – your practical guide to success*, provides detailed guidance for candidates on the interview and how best to handle it. It tells the candidate exactly what to expect, and gives a wealth of useful tips on interview preparation.

Briefly, the interview will comprise a welcome from the panel of assessors, a ten-minute presentation by the candidate, based on the critical analysis that has been submitted, and a period of questioning, on both the presentation and analysis, and on wider issues relating to the candidate's experience and training. There is a special requirement for candidates on the Antiques and Fine Arts pathway, who are obliged to carry out a written valuation and inspection. Candidates on this pathway are advised to consult RICS Membership Operations Department for further information.

From the point of view of the supervisor or counsellor, how can you help your candidate prepare for the final assessment interview? Well, perhaps the best form of preparation here is practice! Encourage your candidate to give a presentation to you, based on their analysis, and to undergo some sample 'questioning'.

With the presentation, check that this does indeed last the required ten minutes – the effects of adrenalin can often make people talk too fast, or cover ground more quickly than they would in a more relaxed setting. Note that the candidate will not simply be reiterating the contents of the critical analysis, but will be giving the panel an overview of it. This could include discussing the reasons for choosing that particular subject, talking about wider issues relating to it, and extrapolating lessons learnt from it.

Ask the candidate to consider different approaches that could be adopted in a similar situation. You may wish to encourage your candidate to have three or four 'extra points' in mind when giving the presentation, which expand the matter contained in the analysis itself, and give them something extra to talk about. It is vital that the candidate can take a 360° view of the project that is the subject of the analysis – the panel may ask questions about it from an unexpected angle. This of course is why it is vital that the candidate has been heavily and thoroughly involved with that particular project.

Moving on from the questioning based around the critical analysis, ask the candidate the kind of questions based on their experience that you imagine the assessment panel would put to them. Remember that the final assessment interview will adopt a 'competence-based' approach (see page 26 for more information on this). In brief, this is an approach based on practical experience. It does not set out simply to test what a candidate knows, but to assess how they can put this knowledge into practice. In essence, it seeks to ask, 'Is the candidate competent in this area?'.

To assess practical competency, the assessors are likely to ask questions such as: 'Give me an example of a time when....', or, 'I see you have been involved in X. Tell me how you went about this.' This approach aims to allow the candidate to demonstrate his or her skills and abilities across the range of competencies covered during the training period.

With those competencies that are required to higher than Level 1, the assessors will aim to move beyond the candidate's firm knowledge and experience, to test their more general attitudes and behaviours (this is known as a part competence-based approach). More details on this type of questioning are provided on page 26.

If you feel you are too intimately involved with the candidate's progress to carry out this questioning objectively, consider asking a colleague to perform this function for you – or at the least, to sit in the room with you while you hold the 'interview', and compare notes later.

A big problem with any interview – and especially one with so much riding on it – can be nerves. There are various techniques for countering these, which are recommended to the candidate in *APC 2006 – your practical guide to success*. Supervisors and counsellors can also help by giving the candidate a chance to practise under 'interview conditions'. Hold a practice interview in a formal setting, in formal dress, with a colleague who is less well-known to the candidate in attendance. Impress on the candidate that if they can survive and 'pass' this experience, then they can succeed in the actual interview.

During the practice interview, ask yourself the following questions:

- Does the candidate's presentation truly reflect the content of the critical analysis, and his or her role in the project chosen?

- Do you have a proper sense of what the candidate has achieved over the training period?

- Can the candidate answer all of your questions properly – or is he or she under-prepared, or answering by rote, in a particular area?

- Would you be happy, if you were an assessor, to admit this candidate to membership of RICS?

If the answer to any of these questions is 'no', then consider exactly what the candidate must do to rectify the situation.

Be ready to give honest feedback to the candidate after holding practice interviews – even on matters as personal as formality of dress, use of eye-contact and body language, speed of speech, your level of interest in the presentation, and their levels of nerves and enthusiasm. Honesty is by far the best policy at this stage in the proceedings. If you do have to make a honest criticism, make sure it is constructive (i.e. tell the candidate what they can do, to put the problem right), and temper it with praise in other areas. A confident candidate is much more likely to be successful than a demoralised candidate. If you've got to this stage in the APC process, then you know they can do it – make sure they know that too.

Finally, do the obvious. Encourage your candidate to have a restful week or so before the interview. Make sure they know where the assessment centre is, and how they will get there.

If you have carefully followed the advice in the rest of this book, your candidate should have nothing to worry about. The final assessment will be simply the formal end to a process of continuous and progressive assessment: the 'stamp of approval' on what has gone before. There is therefore no need for your candidate to feel that everything is riding on this interview, and to build it up into an insurmountable obstacle. By the time of the final interview, it is in fact too late for the candidate to 'save the day' by pulling off a fine performance.

AFTER THE FINAL ASSESSMENT

It is my profound hope that, by following the advice in this book, all of your candidates will pass the final assessment at the first attempt. Sometimes, though, things do go wrong, and candidates are 'referred', allowing them to retake the final assessment six months (or more) afterwards. Referrals are discussed in detail later in this book, in Chapter 8.

BEYOND SUCCESS

Successful candidates are a credit not just to themselves, but to their supervisors and counsellors, and to their firms. Make sure they know that you are proud of their achievement. Encourage them to feel that they have not just 'passed a test', but have taken the first steps into an exciting and fascinating profession. The rest of their career begins here – and hopefully much of it will be spent with the firm that helped them to initial success.

A successful candidate will be a good employee and an advertisement for other good employees. The investment put in by the employer, supervisor and counsellor throughout the APC process will now start to pay off – for all concerned.

A last word of advice

For you to have the confidence that you can guide your candidate correctly, you need to know exactly what you should be doing at each stage in the process. Read, and reread Chapters 3 and 4, to ensure that the process is completely clear in your mind.

Documentation for the APC

5.

In the previous chapters I have mentioned most of the documentation associated with the APC process. In this chapter I would like to look at some of these documents in more detail. It is essential that supervisors and counsellors familiarise themselves with all the documents required, so that they can understand exactly what is required of them and the candidate.

In this chapter, I discuss the following documents:

- enrolment form;
- change of employer form;
- structured training agreement;
- professional development record;
- diary;
- log book;
- achievement record; and
- critical analysis.

Below, I explain what each document is, and what function it performs. There is then a 'practical guidance' section for supervisors and counsellors, explaining their role with regard to each document.

ENROLMENT FORM

An enrolment form is obtainable from RICS Contact Centre:

T +44 (0)870 333 1600

F +44 (0)20 7334 3811

E contactrics@rics.org

W www.rics.org

You and your candidate MUST read the guides carefully. You must send the completed enrolment form with the correct fee, to RICS Membership Operations Enrolment Team. Details of the fees and diary start date are sent with the enrolment form. You must submit all the required material otherwise your enrolment cannot be accepted. Once accepted, RICS will confirm your registration and give you a start date for recording your experience.

A candidate cannot enrol until he or she is in employment – but it is in your interests to get the ball rolling as soon after that as possible, so that you have a fully trained and qualified member of staff as soon as possible.

Before your candidate can reach the final assessment, a minimum of 400 days of experience, within (at least) 24 calendar months, must have been completed for Graduate Route 1 or 200 days in 12 calendar months for Graduate Route 2 candidates. With final assessment interviews only held twice a year (details on www.rics.org), a delay of just a few weeks in enrolling could put the final assessment back by six months.

It is important to take note of the following documents (available on: www.rics.org):

• *APC candidate's guide*;

- *APC/ATC requirements and competencies guide*;
- *APC guide for supervisors, counsellors and employers*; and
- the relevant *APC Pathway Guides*.

The guides contain the various templates that will be needed by the candidate to record his or her training. The APC guide for supervisors, counsellors and employers also contains guidance on the development of a structured training agreement.

Practical guidance

To show the candidate your commitment from the outset, offer to agree a time and date to discuss the application form. You can then provide any necessary support and advice on this, if required. Stress the importance, as noted above, of returning the application documentation promptly. (For more information on the enrolment process, see page 26.)

CHANGE OF EMPLOYER FORM

It is mandatory to keep RICS informed of changes of employer. Candidate's can email contactrics@rics.org with the new details or a 'change of employer' form is available on www.rics.org. This needs to be completed and returned to RICS should the candidate leave your firm's employment during the training period.

Practical guidance

If your firm takes on a new employee who has already enrolled on the APC with another employer, you should check that the appropriate notification has been sent to RICS, giving details of the new employment. Failure to do so may delay the candidate's final assessment, as RICS may not recognise the 'gap' as counting towards the minimum training period.

You may also wish to remind any candidates leaving your employment that this form must be completed and returned to RICS, with details of the new employer.

STRUCTURED TRAINING AGREEMENT

'Structured training' is, as the name suggests, a structured approach to the delivery of training over any given period. All firms registering new APC candidates are obliged to have a structured training agreement in place.

The structured training agreement is simply a document that formalises the intention of the parties to deliver (on the part of the employer) and receive (in respect of the candidate) the training requirements of the chosen APC route over an agreed period and to specified levels of competence.

A pro-forma STA can be downloaded from www.rics.org. The STA must be used in conjunction with the RICS APC guides. It **does not** replace them. In reality, firms that have taken on several APC candidates in the past will already have an agreement in place (although this must be tailored to meet the individual requirements of each candidate) and others will have an agreement that has been approved by RICS.

In general an agreement would be expected to contain the following:

- the role and responsibilities of the supervisor and counsellor;
- information on the employer organisation and areas of activity;
- a statement of the employer's commitment to training, whether they pay for APC/RICS subscriptions, and any time allowed for APC training;
- information on how the required professional development is to be achieved, paying particular attention to the guidance in the APC guides;

- arrangements and key timescales for monitoring the training programme, including regular meetings with supervisor and counsellor, interim and final assessment reports, critical analysis and submissions for final assessment; and

- commitment by the candidate to follow the APC guidance, keep their diary and all other documentation up to date, prepare for meetings with the supervisor and counsellor, and ensure all necessary reports are prepared to agreed timescales.

Practical guidance

For employers who do not have a training agreement in place, the sample agreement and guidance will provide a useful discussion document for the supervisor and candidate to plan and agree the training for the next two years. Supervisors may also approach an RICS training adviser (RTA) for additional support on drawing up the structured training agreement. (For more information on RTAs, see Chapter 9.)

Employers who have recently trained APC candidates will already have a training agreement in place and will be familiar with RICS requirements. All that will be needed is a degree of tailoring to each individual candidate and a note of the proposed training in relation to the timescales and competencies. If this agreement has been discussed and agreed by an RTA, then it is referred to as an 'approved plan'. Again, for more information on how to set up an approved plan, contact RICS or your RTA.

The main advantage of having an 'approved' plan is that it is a demonstration of your commitment to APC training, and may be used when advertising for graduates. It is, if you like, the RICS training advisers' kite-mark of excellence. Additionally, of course, having a plan in place saves time when considering the training plan for each new candidate.

Extracts from a real structured training agreement are provided overleaf.

There sometimes seems to be a view that larger employers stand a better chance of getting candidates through the APC, as they may have more opportunities for the candidate to gain a breadth of experience. I would reassure those working in smaller firms that this is not the case, in my experience. Everything depends on the firm itself. If an employer understands what needs to be done, and takes time to tailor requirements to the candidate's needs, then size is of no issue. A smaller employer, where the candidate is in closer proximity to all other members of staff, and to the decisions being made, may have more scope for flexible development than a candidate in a larger, more impersonal firm, where the training programme may be more rigid.

An acquaintance of mine, in a small practice in the north of England, takes on one graduate every two years – and every two years, that graduate passes the APC. The size of the practice enables the supervisor to take a very personal and close interest in the candidate's progress. Whether this happens in a large or small firm, that approach is the best possible training ground.

When the structured training agreement and competency achievement planner have been drawn up, it must be sent for approval by an RICS Training Advisor. It is not sent to RICS. Once the RTA approves the documents he or she will notify RICS and confirmation will be sent.

A sample structured training agreement is available on www.rics.org.

PROFESSIONAL DEVELOPMENT RECORD

For each 12 months of practical training that is completed, the candidate must also undertake an annual minimum of 48 hours of professional development. The idea behind professional development is that it provides an opportunity for the candidate to acquire some of the additional skills and knowledge that it is not always possible for the employer to provide within the week-to-week business of their practice. This may particularly apply to various of the mandatory competencies.

Professional development should be designed to complement and support the candidate's on-the-job training and development. It may comprise formal training courses or more informal types of learning, such as structured reading, distance learning programmes and secondments. However it should be noted that while structured reading and private study are acceptable they should not form more than two thirds of the total hours required in any 12 months of structured training. While it is the candidate's ultimate responsibility to plan and acquire professional development, it is important that the supervisor and counsellor take an active interest in this and assist with the evaluation.

Like every other aspect of the APC, professional development should be planned and structured, with the aim of completing the requisite number of hours. The 48 hours should reflect the requirements of the candidate's chosen route. So, for example, if the candidate has chosen the Building control pathway to membership, then around 16 hours per year should be allocated for 'technical skills development' linked to the core and optional competencies of this pathway. A further 16 hours should be allocated for 'professional practice skills development', linked to those competencies associated with professional practice, code of ethics and conflicts of interest; with a further 16 hours dedicated to 'skills development' linked to the requirements of the other mandatory competencies. (Advice on how to meet some of these requirements is provided in Chapter 7, where I discuss the mandatory competencies in detail.)

A typical annual plan could look like the example below.

Professional Development for 2007

Technical skills development: linked to core/optional technical competencies – normally 16 hours.

Skills development: linked to mandatory competencies – normally 16 hours.

Professional practice skills development: linked to those competencies associated with professional practice, code of ethics and conflicts of interest – a further 16 hours.

Having decided on the plan, the hours of learning achieved by the candidate are then recorded in Template 3 (professional development record) over the course of the two years of training. This template is checked by the supervisor and counsellor regularly, to ensure that good progress is being made.

Practical guidance

My first piece of advice is to ensure that your candidate understands what counts as 'professional development'.

Professional development is learning what is relevant to the candidate's professional role and learning needs. The most important aspect is the 'learning outcome'. Many activities can qualify not just formal training courses. The candidate's record of professional development should ideally include a balanced mix of formal courses, structured reading and other activities.

The RICS website has a checklist of the type of activities or events from which the candidate might be able to gain a learning outcome (visit www.rics.org). Even this is not a definitive list! Overall, the candidate needs to ensure, when choosing a 'learning activity', that some significant learning occurs.

Remember also that the activities chosen should complement the requirements of the candidate's main area of work. The panel at the final assessment interview will check carefully that there has been a sensible, structured approach to professional development over the training period. There should be a clearly defined relationship between the topics selected for professional development purposes and the competencies. The training suggested for the various mandatory competencies in Chapter 7 may be useful for candidates planning their professional development. With 32 of the 48 hours designed to reflect the mandatory competencies, this may be a useful place to start.

Bear in mind that the 48 hours per year recorded for professional development are over and above the 400 days (200 for Graduate Route 2) to be recorded for the competencies. Although the professional development hours must reflect the requirements of the competencies, the candidate cannot 'double-count' experience. He or she must decide where to record particular experience – under a mandatory competency heading in the log book, or in the professional development record. This should not pose a problem: over the course of 24 months, there is more than enough time to gain the necessary experience in all areas.

If, in discussion with the candidate, you feel that there is a need for variation regarding the number of hours allocated in the typical annual plan shown above, you must ensure that an explanation of this departure from the norm is included in the interim and final summaries of progress. There are many good reasons for such a departure – candidates who are highly experienced in a particular area of work, for example, may spend less time on professional development relating to the core competencies, and more on those relating to the more unfamiliar mandatory competencies.

In the context of life-long learning, the professional development undertaken as a component of the APC is a precursor to the candidate's CPD (continuing professional development) commitments upon qualification. Professional development is essential for all surveyors to continue to grow and learn.

There is more information on the professional development record in Chapter 4.

DIARY

Candidates are obliged to keep a record in a diary to show how their day-to-day training and experience is being built up. This diary may be paper-based, in the form of a desk diary, or may be kept electronically. A diary Template may be found on www.rics.org.

The detail contained in the diary will be used for three specific reasons:

- to complete the log book;

- to help with the signing off of competencies in the forms in the achievement record; and

- to assist with the completion of the interim and final assessment records.

The diary can also be requested by an RTA at any time – so it is important it is always up-to-date.

Practical guidance

Candidates record their experience in the diary with reference to their achievement against the competencies. Entries should be fairly detailed: a half-day entry stating simply 'valuation of commercial property' will not help in preparing the interim or final assessment records, nor with preparation for the final assessment. However, an entry noting: 'valued a shop at [insert address] for rent review purposes, file reference [XXXX]. Large, double-fronted shop in secondary location, with good service access and parking to rear. Modern lease with no onerous clauses or provisions' will provide the candidate with a memory-jogger for those reports and for preparation for the final assessment.

LOG BOOK

The log book (Template 2) must be completed by the candidate every month. The log book is a summary of the candidate's diary, showing the training – in number of days – grouped under the competency headings. In practice, it is a good idea for candidates to complete their log book at more regular intervals, preferably at the end of each week.

The log book will be sent to RICS as part of the final assessment submission, to be used by the assessment panel. The information it contains is very useful to the assessors, as it provides an immediate snapshot of the candidate's areas of work experience. In conjunction with the forms in the achievement record it will be used to structure the final assessment interview to obtain the correct balance of questioning relative to the candidate's experience.

Practical guidance

It is vital that candidates achieve the right balance of days recorded against each of the competencies. The number of days for each competency will be looked at closely by the final assessment panels, when they examine the log book.

The minimum training requirement is for 400 days over 24 calendar months for Graduate Route 1 or 200 days over 12 months for Graduate Route 2 candidates. Bear in mind that mandatory competencies are not recorded as part of the 400/200 days, but must be mentioned in the final assessment record.

In any 12 months a typical candidate might work for around 45–46 weeks, or 220–230 days. So in theory, the requirement of 400 days can quite easily be met. The example on page 68 indicates how experience can be shared out between the competencies.

One of the main points of confusion when allocating days concerns the mandatory competencies. A lot of the training and experience needed to achieve the mandatory competencies will be acquired as part of the training and experience for the core and optional competencies. For example, health and safety, customer care and communication skills are all likely to be addressed when carrying out training for almost any core or optional competency.

Some formal training may of course also occur for the mandatory competencies, delivered in full days, and this may be mentioned in your candidate's final assessment record as such. An example of this would be health and safety training forming part of a firm's induction programme. Or, for example, the candidate may spend a whole day dealing with a complaint, and decide to record this as experience to Level 2 of the Client care mandatory competency.

The fact that one day is just one day, and must be recorded as such even if it fulfils two different requirements, should not prove a handicap to the candidate. There is plenty of time over the course of the two years to fulfil all the various time requirements. There will also, of course, be an overlap between the core and optional competencies. Training for one will be gained in the course of training for another. A commonsense approach is once again needed with regard to apportioning the time spent on each competency in the diary.

Note that professional development hours are recorded in Template 3, and not the log book. Again, it may be necessary for the candidate to make a decision as to where exactly to allocate days and hours of experience, if there is an overlap in the requirements.

Overall, both the candidate, and the supervisor and counsellor, must appreciate that training and experience rarely breaks down neatly into categories. Candidates will be learning all the time – it is just a case of deciding where and how best to record the experience. Experience in one area helps to build experience in another. Even if it cannot be recorded in two categories, it is never wasted.

One final piece of advice is not to attempt to cover too many competencies over the training period, thus spreading the candidate's experience thinly over too many areas. This rule is particularly applicable to candidates completing the APC in the 400-day/24-month minimum training period. The situation may be more relaxed if the candidate is carrying out the APC over a longer period.

Sample breakdown of days: Valuation pathway

There are 10 mandatory competencies for this pathway. Six are required to Level 1, three to Level 2 and one to Level 3. For Graduate Route 1 candidates I would suggest ascribing a maximum 1 day to each of the Level 1 competencies, and 14 days to the remainder, over the course of the two years.

In the Valuation pathway there are three core competencies: Valuation to Level 3; Inspection to Level 3; and Measurement of Land and Property to Level 2. There is then a minimum of two optional competencies to Level 3 and one competency to Level 2 from a 'closed' list of competencies which have been put together by the valuation faculty. This list may be found on page 16 of the July 2006 *APC/ATC requirements and competencies guide*.

In addition, candidates must also complete one competency to level 3 or two competencies to level 2 from the full list of technical competencies, and this may include any not already chosen from the 'closed' list shown on page 16 of the *APC/ATC requirements and competencies guide*.

This equates to a minimum of seven competencies at 19 levels or eight competencies at 20 levels.

If we take the example of 20 levels, then the division into 400 days gives around 20 days per level of competency.

On the basis of the total diary entries recorded over the two-year period, a breakdown might look as follows.

Mandatory competencies	20 days
Core competencies	
Valuation	100 days
Inspection	40 days
Measurement	40 days
Optional competencies	
Capital taxation (Level 3)	60 days
Local taxation/assessment (Level 3)	60 days
Landlord and Tenant (including rent reviews and lease renewals) (Level 2)	40 days
Plus	
Compulsory acquisition and compensation (Level 3)	60 days
Core total	400 days

For the core competencies, I have placed the emphasis on Valuation, which is key to this pathway, and reduced the number of days for Inspection and Measurement, which are less onerous.

The above is of course just for example and is in no way prescriptive. Hopefully it illustrates my main point, which is that the key issue is to show a balance across the competencies.

For Graduate Route 2 candidates previous experience may mean that they reach the required level of one compentency much quicker than another.

ACHIEVEMENT RECORD

The achievement record comprises a collection of documents:

- templates 4 and 5, for signing off the mandatory core and optional competencies;

- the three-monthly supervisor reports (template on www.rics.org), which are not submitted to RICS;

- the six-monthly counsellor reports (template on www.rics.org), which are not submitted to RICS; and

- the interim and final assessment records; templates 6,7 and 8 (which include a declaration of completion of interim assessment).

Practical guidance

Templates 4 and 5

It is in Templates 4 and 5 that the supervisor and counsellor 'sign off' the candidate as having achieved the appropriate level in the various competencies. The templates are reviewed at the three- and six-monthly reviews. A discussion should take place at these reviews around each of the competencies, and the supervisor can then take a view as to whether any of the competencies should be signed off, and at what level this should occur. To sign off a competency, the supervisor should date and initial the appropriate box. The counsellor then likewise dates and initials the appropriate boxes at the six-monthly reviews, if satisfied that the candidate has indeed reached the appropriate level of competence.

Templates 6, 7 and 8

The three- and six-monthly reports, and all the documents contained in the interim and final assessment records, are discussed in detail in Chapter 4, under the appropriate chronological headings.

CRITICAL ANALYSIS

The critical analysis is a written report of a maximum of 3,000 words, comprising a detailed analysis of a project, or projects, with which the candidate has been extensively involved over the training period. Chapter 4 discusses in detail the choice of subject for the analysis.

The aim of the analysis is to give the assessors firm evidence of the candidate's ability to work effectively and within the competency requirements. The analysis should indicate a thorough understanding of each project concerned and the processes that were followed. In the final assessment, the candidate will be questioned on the approach outlined in the analysis, as well as on wider issues surrounding the report. It is therefore vital that the candidate has a good all-round view of each project.

The conclusion of the analysis should include a critical appraisal of the project(s), together with some reflective analysis of the lessons learnt and experience gained.

The main failing of critical analyses that do not satisfy the assessors is a lack of early preparation. The choice of subject is either too simplistic or is not a reflection of what the candidate has been doing during the training period. Remember that the analysis must be a reflection of the candidate's own work, and of something in which they have been directly and heavily involved.

Another common failing is omitting to follow the guidance in terms of the format of the report, as set out in the *APC Candidate's Guide*.

To summarise this, the analysis must be word-processed and must be a maximum of 3,000 words (not including the appendices). It is advisable to include photographs and plans, which must be no larger than A4 size when folded. It must be signed and dated by the candidate, and certified by the supervisor and counsellor. Critical analyses are sometimes received by the final assessment panel in such a dog-eared, scruffy, unbound state that it seems inconceivable that a supervisor or counsellor can have properly looked at them. The standard of presentation should be as high as for any other report leaving your office and representing your firm.

Official guidance calls for the critical analysis to fall under the following headings:

- Key issues;

- Options (to include reasons for rejecting options that may not be feasible);

- Your proposed solution; and

- Conclusion and analysis of the experience gained.

It is vital that all these headings exist, and that the commentary under them is relevant to each one. When covering more than one project, candidates are likely to find it sensible to repeat the headings (or most of them) for their analysis of each project. Too often, analysis is written in the style of a report to a client, and becomes too much of a 'diary of events'. Lateral thought is missing, there is no critical appraisal or reflective analysis, and the report therefore fails.

Supervisors and counsellors should also make sure that the analysis allows the candidate to demonstrate ability across the various competencies. To do so, it is not necessary to formally list each competency and discuss how this has been covered, but simply to step back and consider what exactly it is the candidate has done, and how this fits with the requirements of the competencies. If this is clear to you, it should be clear to the final assessment panel too.

There is further guidance available for candidates on the critical analysis in the *APC Candidate's Guide*, as well as in the RICS Books publication, *APC 2006 – your practical guide to success.*

Once the analysis is written, the best help that a supervisor and counsellor can give a candidate is to stand in the shoes of an assessor. Ask the candidate to provide you with a first draft and check that the key issues referred to above are covered. Consider the layout, presentation, spelling and grammar – are these of a high standard? Stand back and analyse the technical and professional impact: are you satisfied that it is truly representative of your candidate's work, and that it meets with the required level of the appropriate competencies?

The candidate will be required, at the final assessment interview, to give a ten-minute presentation on the analysis.

A last word of advice

Two years is a long time – records and documentation can become scruffy and dog-eared in that time. However, it is always a good idea, wherever possible, to hand in original records. Assessors may well be suspicious of records that have been redone, or tidied up, and all re-signed with the same dates.

6. The competencies

WHAT ARE THE COMPETENCIES?

The APC is a test which ensures that trainee surveyors are competent in terms of the standards set by RICS. To be 'competent' is to have the skill or ability to perform a task or function – this ability can vary from being merely able, to being expert in a particular sphere of activity.

A 'competency' is a statement of the skills or abilities required to perform a specific task or function. It is based upon attitudes and behaviours, as well as skills and knowledge. The training structure of the APC requires candidates to achieve a certain set of competencies. These are a mix of technical and professional practice, interpersonal, financial, business and management skills.

The competencies a candidate undertakes depend on the pathway to membership being followed. The *APC/ATC requirements and competencies guide* sets out the required competencies and levels of attainment for each APC Pathway – candidates, supervisors and counsellors must all read this guide carefully.

In a broader context, the use of competency-based assessment is fast becoming a worldwide phenomenon. It is felt that such an approach results in candidates and employees who have not just theoretical knowledge, but the ability to put this into practice. The basic philosophy behind competency-based assessment is that evidence of 'past performance' and behaviour is the best prediction of future performance and behaviour.

LIST AND LEVELS OF COMPETENCIES

The *APC/ATC requirements and competencies guide* sets out what the candidate needs to achieve by way of skills and abilities over the training period. It notes the requirements of each APC Pathway, with a list of the number of competencies to be covered during the training period and the level of attainment required in each. The guide also includes the full list of competencies in alphabetical order, giving each a reference number for use on the achievement record and spelling out precisely what each entails.

The competencies cover three levels of attainment, which are progressive in terms of skills and abilities:

- Level 1 – Knowledge and understanding of the areas covered by the competency;

- Level 2 – Application of this knowledge and understanding in practical situations; and

- Level 3 – Ability to provide reasoned advice and depth of technical knowledge.

Depth of technical knowledge referred to in level 3, for a Graduate Route 1 candidate, must be viewed in the context of the level of experience a candidate can reasonably be expected to achieve after just two years. Candidates will reach each level in a progressive and logical order – as the above should indicate, it is not possible to move from Level 1 to 3 without passing through Level 2.

Consider the example opposite of the building surveying competency of 'building pathology', which progresses in complexity across the levels.

Building pathology

Level 1: demonstrate your knowledge and understanding of building defects including collection of information, measurements and tests.

Level 2: apply your knowledge to undertake surveys, use survey and other information to diagnose cause and mechanisms of failure;

Level 3: Provide evidence of reasoned advice and appropriate recommendations, including the preparation and presenting reports

A typical final assessment question for this competency might be:

'I notice from your summaries of experience that you have carried out building surveys on a number of traditionally built 1960s houses. Describe how you went about those surveys [Level 1]. What were the common types of failure to brickwork observed while carrying out those inspections? What were the causes and how did you diagnose these? [Level 2]. What method of repair did you recommend to your client, and why? What sort of issues did you include in your final report and recommendations? [Level 3].'

The levels of competencies are discussed in more detail below.

TYPES OF COMPETENCIES

The APC has three types of competencies: mandatory, core and optional. The core and optional competencies are referred to as 'technical' competencies.

The mandatory competencies are considered by RICS to underpin all practice as a chartered surveyor. All candidates on all pathways must achieve these.

The core competencies are the primary skills of the candidate's chosen pathway. For example, 'Valuation' is a core competency in the Valuation pathway. Similarly, 'Contract practices' is a core competency in the Quantity Surveying and Construction pathway.

The optional competencies are selected by the candidate as additional requirements for the chosen pathway. For each pathway, the candidate must achieve all of the core competencies, and a certain number of optional competencies. The optional competencies are not so called because they are optional altogether – the candidate has a choice of which.

You will note from the *APC/ATC requirements and competencies guide* that with most pathways candidates will start by selecting optional competencies from a closed list, and then there is a further requirement based on the full list of technical competencies including any already not chosen from the 'closed' list. It is important that the guidance notes for each pathway (as set out in the *APC/ATC requirements and competencies guide* available on www.rics.org) are considered carefully so as to ensure the correct selection of competencies.

HOW DOES THE CANDIDATE CHOOSE THE COMPETENCIES?

First of all, remember that all candidates must achieve the mandatory competencies – there is no choice in that.

The other competencies are chosen by reference to the candidate's APC pathway. On enrolment, the candidate, in conjunction with his or her employer, selects the pathway (from the 21 available) – there will be a pathway guide to provide more detailed information.

The new *APC/ATC Pathway Guides*, available on www.rics.org, further illuminate the experience requirements within each of the competencies. Set out below is an explanation of the experience required in the Building pathology competency taken from the Building Surveying pathway guide and gives further guidance on the areas of experience that a candidate will be expected to cover.

Building pathology

Level 1: Demonstrate knowledge and understanding of:

- typical defects relating to typical buildings found in your locality that you may have come across and explain cause and effect of these;

- building defects likely to be encountered in typical building surveying activities, e.g. wet and dry rot, flat roof defects, concrete defects, etc.;

- the various methods to collect, store and retrieve information for various differing purposes when carrying out property inspections;

- the various different types of inspection that may be carried out and the importance of accurate recording of information during inspection; and

- differing types of testing and the limitations of the tests, e.g. the use of damp meters and borescopes.

Level 2:

- explain in detail cause and mechanics of varying types of failure;

- explain procedures for carrying out inspections of properties;

- be able to explain, using detailed examples, the relationship between observations taken on site and the diagnosis of failure in building fabric;

- be able to use examples, from your own experience, to demonstrate your application of knowledge gained at Level 1; and

- be able to use knowledge and information gathered from several sources, including if necessary specialist inspections to diagnose and explain building fabric failure

Level 3:

- prepare reports for clients, explaining in non-technical language the causes of failure and the likely results of failure, together with the appropriate remedial measures;

- using information gathered from inspections formulate the necessary remedial/preventative works including specific detail in the form of a schedule of works if required;

- show an understanding of the level of detail required in typical reports, including examples of layout and the use of sketches, drawings and photographs;

- be able to discuss in detail examples of unusual defects you have been involved with and remedial works employed; and

- be able to demonstrate the differing requirements of reports to clients, e.g. the differences between schedules of condition, schedules of dilapidations and pre-acquisition reports.

A special note on the Research pathway

Candidates following the Research pathway will note that there are no optional competency requirements set out in the *APC/ATC requirements and competencies guide*. In the special notes for this pathway, it states that candidates are required to demonstrate competence in the research that is applied to the delivery of solutions to a wide range of projects, employing a range of approaches and relating to a number of locations. The research must be relevant to the candidate's chosen pathway. Therefore, for example, if a Research pathway candidate is working in a 'commercial property' firm, he or she will need to be signed off to Level 1 in five core and optional competencies from the Commercial Property Practice pathway.

There is an additional requirement that the candidate must also demonstrate competence in one competency to level 2 and two competencies to level 1 from the full list of technical competencies.

Conclusion

It is clear from the above that candidates must select competencies that enable them to attain the full range of primary skills, guided by the relevant Pathway Guide. Candidates should not be tempted to select what they might see as an 'easy choice' of competency.

If further guidance is needed, candidates should first consult their supervisor and counsellor, and then approach an RTA, an APC Doctor or the RICS Membership Operations Department.

Overall, the combination of competencies must reflect the day-to-day work the candidate carries out with his or her employer. The candidate's judgment in choosing the competencies will be taken into account at the final assessment interview. The assessors will expect the candidate to have made a realistic and sensible choice, reflecting the skills needed to practise as a surveyor within their chosen field.

WHAT DO THE COMPETENCIES ENTAIL?

The *APC/ATC requirements and competencies guide* sets out the competencies in two lists: Mandatory and

Technical (core and optional). Both lists are in alphabetical order and give each competency a specific reference.

Each competency is then discussed in more detail (except for Ethics, professional identity and accountability, which is covered in detail on page 5 of the guide). The requirements for each level are noted. Readers of the list will quickly realise that the competencies are set out in a generic way, so that they can be applied to different areas of practice and geographical location. It is important that they are interpreted within the context of the candidate's own area of practice and specialism.

It is obviously impossible to give specific 'one size fits all' guidance on the type of training to be given for each competency. The competencies have been written with a view to flexibility and to allowing the candidate's training to reflect the markets in which they are working. For more detailed guidance on what is expected read the *APC Pathway Guides*. These provide an in depth look at training and experience required.

In general, though, I would suggest that you need to consider providing training and experience which would reflect your firm's expectations of performance by a young graduate after two years at work.

SIGNING OFF THE COMPETENCIES

Supervisors and counsellors express their confidence in a candidate's ability in a particular competency by 'signing off' the competency in the achievement record (Templates 4 and 5).

It is vital that before signing a candidate off at any level, you carefully study the wording of the particular competency and the further explanation set out in the relevant Pathway Guide. You must be satisfied that the candidate has acquired the appropriate experience and will be able to answer questions on the competency at the final assessment interview. Even more importantly, you must be satisfied that his or her achievement in a particular area was not a 'one-off' – you must be confident that they would be able to replicate it at another time, under different circumstances. The point at which a candidate is competent is when you are confident that they could do this, without supervision, to a standard that is acceptable to you. Bear in mind that not only will a candidate not thank you for finding that he or she has been wrongly signed off at too high a level of competence, but you risk lowering the standards of the profession overall.

In deciding at which point a candidate has achieved a particular level of attainment in any of the competencies, there is no minimum number of days of experience required (although I provide some guidance on this in Chapter 4). In discussion with your candidate, a decision should be made as to when the required level of skill and ability in any particular competency has been reached. The number of days taken to reach the appropriate level will be dependent on a combination of the following factors:

- the starting point – has the candidate any previous experience in the area?;

- the candidate's aptitude and speed of learning in the competency;

- the quality of the training and experience provided; and

- the difficulty of the particular competency.

Base your judgments on notes you have kept and observations you have made (either directly or indirectly, if your candidate is in another department or on a secondment). You may also rely on evidence and samples of work produced by the candidate. You should, of course, discuss aspects of the competency or level with the candidate, questioning his or her depth of understanding.

With regard to signing off the core competencies, you should think of these as being progressive over the whole course of the training period, with experience being gained over the full 24 months for Graduate Route 1 or 12 months for a Graduate Route 2 candidate. The optional competencies tend to be specialist topics and more focused. These may be achieved over a 12-month period.

The mandatory competencies need to be carefully planned over the 24-month training period. Candidates have ten areas to cover, and it may be useful to aim to achieve, say, four or five mandatory competencies in the first year and the remainder in the second year. A balanced approach is necessary. The conduct rules, ethics and professional practice competence, required to Level 3, may cover the full 24 months, whereas more specialist or specific competencies, many of which are only required to Level 1, may be achieved in a much shorter period of time.

Always check that the candidate feels confident in the competency at the level being discussed before you sign it off. After 24 months, and in the very early part of their career, candidates cannot be expected to know everything. Some of the levels in some of the competencies represent huge areas of knowledge and experience, which may take a long time to acquire. Take, for example, the Quantity surveying competency of Contract Practice (ref T017), which relates to the various forms of contract used in the construction industry. This is a huge area, covering many forms and types of contract, and ranging from the small works types of contract used in civil projects to some very specialist contracts covering mechanical and electrical equipment and similar, with some of these being very geographically specific.

Another example of a vast area is the Building pathology competency (ref T006), which covers a huge range of materials, buildings and specific aspects of construction (foundations, walls, roofs, and so on). It is important to realise that learning in these competencies can span a lifetime. You therefore need to be realistic in your expectations as to what can be covered in a 24-month period.

In both examples there is plenty of further information set out in the respective Pathway Guides.

It should also be noted that, in the above examples, although candidates may not have had hands-on experience in a particular area, they are still expected to have some knowledge and understanding of the issues, in order to meet the requirements of the competency. In the Quantity surveying example above, the candidate may only have had experience of one or two types of contract, but will still need a general knowledge and understanding of others. With the Building pathology example, the candidate may have worked solely in housing and traditional brick-type construction, but will still need a knowledge and understanding of other types of building and forms of construction.

As a final word of advice, think of your role as that of someone who has the ability to 'stand back' from the day-to-day training process, in order to consider what the candidate has achieved. From his or her point of view, a new candidate may simply have carried out a day's valuation. The supervisor and counsellor must be able to break down that day's work into its constituent factors, and apply these to the competency requirements, to help the candidate understand how that day contributes towards the requirements of the core, optional and mandatory competencies.

Levels 1, 2 and 3

The differences between Levels 1 and 2 of each competency are usually fairly straightforward. Level 1 requires in the main, a knowledge and understanding of a particular subject or competency. Level 2 goes on to demand some practical experience – words such as 'to undertake' or 'to carry out' occur in the competency descriptions at this level.

The difference between Levels 2 and 3 is a little more complex. Level 2 can be considered to be an application of knowledge or understanding in normal, everyday circumstances. Level 3 aims to extend this application to giving reasoned advice and more in depth technical knowledge. This difference is highlighted in the Valuation competency at Level 3; the first part of the competency statement calls for candidates to be able to 'demonstrate practical competence in a range of property types or for a range of purposes and to demonstrate the application of a wide range of valuation methods and techniques'. This does not mean that someone with 24 months of experience needs to be able to value an oil refinery or a steelworks – but it does mean that they should have had some experience in a valuation that is more complex than usual. They should also have experience of providing advice to clients.

The 'signing off' process should be progressive across the levels. Competency levels should be reached gradually over the training period, and not within days of each other. In addition, the number of days spent reaching a particular level should be reasonable – a candidate is, for example, unlikely to reach Level 3 in Valuation as a result of just six diary training days. It is also important that supervisors adopt a balanced approach to the task, and do not sign all of the competencies off on the same date. Assessors naturally become suspicious when this occurs.

FINAL ASSESSMENT INTERVIEW: ASSESSING THE COMPETENCIES

In the final assessment interview, not only will the candidate be asked direct questions about particular competencies, but the wider questions asked will enable the assessors to take several competencies into account. The assessors will likewise analyse the documentation received from the candidate, particularly the critical analysis, and will watch the presentation closely, to ensure that the requirements of the competencies have been met.

The competencies will be tested at the appropriate level. So, for example, for a Level 1 competency, a candidate might be asked some general questions about inspection, measurement, surveys, or similar. A typical example from the Rural pathway would be for a candidate to discuss a valuation of a farm in which he or she was involved. The candidate might be asked to explain how he or she went about the inspection of the farm, its buildings, land and crops.

For Level 2, the assessor might question the candidate in some detail as to how he or she prepared the valuation, discussing some of the problems or issues that were encountered. The underlying question for Level 2 is: 'How did you apply your knowledge in this area in a practical way?'.

Level 3 seeks to extend this further, asking the candidate to look at a particular aspect in a wider context, with questions such as: 'What were the implications of your approach? What other things might have impacted on your actions or this situation?' The assessor will thus step outside of the candidate's direct experience, perhaps posing a theoretical problem. Continuing the Rural example, the candidate might be asked how he or she would deal with a valuation if it was discovered that a farm was trading at a loss.

It is the questioning at Level 3 that makes the final assessment a 'part' competence-based interview, rather than wholly competence-based. Level 3 aims to extend the questioning beyond the candidate's direct experience, into the wider areas surrounding this experience.

To prepare your candidate for this type of questioning, you should, in your three- and six-monthly reviews, ask similar questions, to encourage a widening of knowledge and understanding. Test your candidate's understanding of the whole work environment, asking questions and setting problems that draw on his or her previous experience, and then stretch this a little further. It is a particularly good idea to employ this approach for some of the mandatory competencies. A candidate with two years' experience, for example, may well have had no personal involvement with an issue relating to ethics or the Rules of Conduct. However, he or she must still have a firm knowledge of what is required in this regard, and the ability to think more widely – and possibly hypothetically – in this area.

More information on the type of questions likely to be encountered by candidates (including examples) is provided in the RICS Books publication, *APC 2006 – your practical guide to success.*

A last word of advice

Competencies are practical, not theoretical. They allow the assessors to ensure that the candidate is 'competent' to practice. Make sure that you do not sign-off a candidate if you suspect that achievement in any competency was a 'one-off'. The candidate must be competent to repeat the achievement under other circumstances.

7. The mandatory competencies

The minimum standards for mandatory competencies set out in the *APC/ATC requirements and competencies guide* have been set by the Education Membership Committee. These competencies are structured in levels.

Your candidate must achieve the minimum standards, as follows:

Conduct Rules, ethics and professional practice	To Level 3
Client Care Communication and negotiation Health and safety	To Level 2
Accounting principles and procedures Business planning Conflict avoidance, management and dispute resolution procedures Data management Sustainability Team working	To Level 1

All of the above competencies are defined in a discrete section of the *APC/ATC requirements and competencies guide*.

In addition, candidates following the Senior Professional Route must achieve the following three competencies:

- leadership (to Level 2);

- managing people (to Level 2);

- managing resources (to Level 2).

The minimum standards described above may also be included at a higher level, if appropriate to the particular pathway. If a pathway includes a mandatory competency to a higher level, this will also appear in the core or optional competency list for that pathway, to the higher level.

Overall, my advice regarding mandatory competencies is that when considering your candidates structured training agreement, you should sort out how you propose to help your candidate achieve the required core and optional competencies, and then sift through the list of mandatory competencies.

Identify the mandatory competencies where you will provide the appropriate training within your candidates day-to-day work, as part of their structured training. This will leave a remainder which will require you and your candidate to consider additional learning or a specific training course. These actions will qualify for your candidates professional development.

MANDATORY COMPETENCIES – IN DETAIL

I would now like to explore the mandatory competencies in more detail. Experience suggests that while the other types of competencies tend to be easily understood by practitioners in the field, there is some confusion in the area of the mandatory requirements. My view is that the mandatory competencies are one of the most important parts of the whole APC. The skills and abilities they encourage and test underpin all professional and technical aspects of working as a surveyor, and are vital for further advancement in the profession.

This chapter will do two things: first, give some further explanation of the requirements for each competency; and second, provide some practical advice on how to help your candidate achieve the required levels, working through the levels outlined. The advice is not intended to be all-encompassing or definitive in any way – each candidate, each pathway, and each firm will alter the ingredients of each competency slightly. It is certainly not possible to say, 'follow this, and you will pass'. What follows are simply suggestions and pointers as to how the requirements of the competencies might be met. In particular, you should note that the recommended reading is not exhaustive – it is, in the main, a selection of some of my favourite texts. Each pathway will have its own specialist authors and texts, and you should use your experience to recommend some reading that in your view will be more tailored to your candidate's pathway.

Some of the training I suggest for the mandatory competencies – particularly the structured reading – may also prove useful for the candidate's professional development purposes. Remember that some 32 hours of professional development a year must be focused around the areas of the mandatory competencies (16 hours on mandatory competencies and a further 16 hours on professional practice). In particular, you may wish to use the RICS online service – isurv (www.isurv.co.uk). This service, mixing expert commentary with official RICS guidance, covers a huge range of surveying matters, and can be used for professional development purposes.

The minimum requirements for the competencies in the mandatory competency list vary from Level 1 to Level 3. Where a competency is required to a level higher than 1, I will explain how to move from one level to the next.

Remember it is important for your candidate to achieve the required levels in a progressive manner. They cannot just achieve Level 3 from a standing start so it is important that they understand the requirements at each level.

CONDUCT RULES, ETHICS AND PROFESSIONAL PRACTICE

Details of this competency are set out on page 30 of the *APC/ATC requirements and competencies guide* with further guidance on page 32. For the purposes of recording in your achievement record, this competency has been given the reference M005. The required level of achievement is 3.

The new RICS Rules of Conduct were released 4 June 2007. There are now two versions of the rules (one for members setting out individual obligations and the other for firms setting out firms' obligations), with supporting policies and non-mandatory help sheets as well as additional guidance available for members of the public. APC candidates will need to familiarise themselves with all three aspects to Level 3. I recommend visiting www.rics.org/newregulation as a first step for any candidate.

Practical guidance

Level 1

The knowledge and understanding required of the candidate at Level 1 is wide-ranging. It covers the role, function and significance of RICS; an understanding of society's expectations of professional practice; RICS Rules of Conduct; and the general principles of law and the legal system, as applicable in their area of practice. The RICS Rules of Conduct are available on www.rics.org/newregulation. The Rules are now principles-based and are not too detailed. Candidates should read the core areas. Some of the key areas are as follows:

- professional indemnity insurance;
- handling clients' money;
- lifelong learning; and
- avaoiding conflicts of interest.

To understand the role and function of RICS, your candidate should carry out some reading around the structure of RICS, the various faculties, faculty boards and committees, and the functions performed, such as advising the government on housing, taxation, planning and landlord and tenant issues, and bringing an influence to bear on all relevant aspects of society. Apart from keeping abreast of developments in newspapers, a good source of information is the RICS magazine, RICS Business, and the various other weekly 'property' publications.

The other requirement at Level 1 involves the candidate understanding the role of the professional person and of society's expectations of such a person. This relationship has been usefully articulated in medical law in the context of doctor/patient relationships. The training period principles of professional integrity hold good in all professional-client situations. An important issue was that of 'ethics', which have been defined as a set of moral principles extending beyond a formal code of conduct.

RICS expects members to act both within the Rules of Conduct and ethically, when delivering surveying services to clients. This approach has been enunciated as RICS 'principles' and is set out as 12 standards (see www.rics.org/newregulation for more detail):

1 Act honourably;

2 Act with integrity;

3 Be open and transparent in your dealings;

4 Be accountable for all your actions;

5 Know and act within your limitations;

6 Be objective at all times;

7 Always treat others with respect;

8 Set a good example;

9 Have the courage to make a stand;

10 Comply with relevant laws and regulations;

11 Avoid conflicts of interest; and

12 Respect confidentiality.

Level 2

Level 2 in this competency requires your candidate to provide evidence of practical application in their area of practice, being able to justify actions at all times and demonstrate personal commitment to the Rules of Conduct, ethics and the help sheet on maintaining professional and ethical standards (available from www.rics.org/newregulation).

Level 3

At Level 3, your candidate should be able to provide evidence of the application of the above in their area of practice in the context of advising clients.

Further guidance

This particular mandatory competency is a huge and expansive topic – but it should be kept in perspective. The final assessment panel will keep their testing and questioning within the confines of the knowledge and experience that a young person, perhaps in their early 20s and occupying a fairly junior position, will have gained. Therefore your candidate will not be expected to have first-hand experience of some of the more detailed areas of the Rules of Conduct for firms, such as your firm's professional indemnity insurance or the details of your clients' money.

The assessment panel's approach will be pitched at some of the areas in which your candidate should have practical experience, such as conflicts of interest and terms of engagement. However, it will also test their wider knowledge around some of the basics, such as why a professional institution has Rules of Conduct, an understanding of the basic principles of professional indemnity insurance and clients' money, and other aspects of the help sheet on maintaining professional and ethical standards (available from www.rics.org/newregulation). Their training should incorporate a mixture of practical experience, structured reading and perhaps some CPD-type events on current issues. This competency is obviously also an ideal subject for their professional development.

The *APC candidate's guide* recommends that training in this area accounts for 16 of the 48 hours per year of professional development experience required.

Levels 2 and 3 will involve you developing your candidate's practical experience at work, with an emphasis on taking instructions, understanding and dealing with conflicts of interest, and applying the 12 standards.

At your three-monthly and six-monthly reviews, you should discuss this with your candidate. You may wish to consider three main areas:

- the role and function of RICS: 'What have they read about RICS activities in recent months?'

- the help sheet on maintaining professional and ethical standards: Test your candidate with questions like 'Give me an example of a time at which you have had to know and act within your limitations?'; 'Tell me about an occasion when you had to have the courage to make a stand?'

- Rules of Conduct: 'What have you read this quarter ... and what do you understand about the Rules of Conduct concerning clients' money/or similar?'

Another useful piece of information is the RICS Professional Regulation and Consumer Protection annual reports which review the year in question and provide information on such topics as compliance, monitoring, disciplinary matters and various useful reports and updates on current issues appropriate in the subject of professional regulation and consumer protection.

RICS Regulation has also published a series of documents on professional practice matters:

- Professional Ethics guidance note: Part 1 introduction

- Professional Ethics guidance note: Part 2 case studies

These guidance notes can be obtained from RICS Regulation on 020 7695 1670 or from www.rics.org. They should be essential reading for every candidate.

Finally, of course, ensure that they can provide evidence of this competency in the interim and final assessment reports – giving examples of structured reading and training and also of practical experience.

CLIENT CARE

Details of this competency are set out on page 29 of the *APC/ATC requirements and competencies guide*. It has the reference M003 for the purposes of recording in the achievement record. This competency is required to be achieved to Level 2. At Level 1, your candidate should be able to demonstrate a knowledge and understanding of the principle and practice of client care including:

- the concept of identifying clients, colleagues and third parties who are your clients and understand the behaviours that are appropriate to establish good client relationships;

- the systems and procedures that are appropriate for managing the process of client care including complaints; and

- the requirements to collect data, analyse and define the needs of clients.

At Level 2, they should be able to apply all of the above in their area of business or practice on a routine basis.

Practical guidance

Approaches to client care will vary from business to business, depending on the nature of the work, the degree of client interface and the type of organisation. At one extreme – residential valuation, sales and letting – there is a high degree of customer interface, and the skill of managing and influencing clients is vital, with the business relying solely on fee income for survival. In areas of central or local government, by contrast, the link is not so direct and the dependency on fee income from transactions not as great. However, one key concept is fundamental to all business: the client is sovereign. Notice that this is not the same as saying, 'the customer is always right' – in surveying matters this is not always the case. Candidates must be able to understand the link between customer care and duty of care. If a client wishes to do something that would be impractical, or impossible, or doomed to certain failure, the surveyor owes the client a duty of care to inform him or her of that. To give the best customer care, your candidate must therefore have a good understanding of each client's needs.

This is one of those competencies where the candidate must be able to 'step back' out of a situation, to analyse what it is that they have learnt about customer care and duty of care in any particular instance. In preparation for the final assessment, they should be able to explain a situation in which they have delivered good client care in the context of their work. You should discuss this with your candidate and provide opportunities where they can develop skills in this area.

To assist their understanding of this subject, the candidate may also wish to undertake some structured reading and training. An excellent textbook on this subject is In *Search of Excellence*, published by Warner Books in 1998. This book looks at a list of top performing companies and examines what it is that leads to excellence – concluding, of course, that it is customer care. It is also essential that your candidate is familiar with RICS complaint handling procedures

COMMUNICATION AND NEGOTIATION

Details of this competency are set out on page 30 of the *APC/ATC requirements and competencies guide*. For the purposes of recording in the achievement record, it has been given the reference M004. It is required to Level 2.

At Level 1, candidates are required to demonstrate a knowledge and understanding of effective oral, written, graphic and presentation skills, including methods and techniques appropriate to specific situations. At Level 2, they are required to provide evidence of practical application of oral, written, graphic and presentation skills that are appropriate in a variety of situations, specifically where negotiation is involved.

Oral communication is used in a wide range of surveying situations and circumstances: at meetings, in negotiations, when managing people, when making presentations, in tenders, and so on. It will include the use of email and of internal memos and letters, for all of which an essential component is being able to write good, unambiguous prose.

In my experience, there is some basic best practice for all situations. This can then be tailored to meet the requirements of specific situations. The list of specific situations is of course huge, and training will also be wide and varied.

Communication skills can be taught formally. A wealth of bodies run courses in this area – these may include, for example, assertiveness training courses. I would suggest, however, that for most candidates, the best approach is to be coached by senior people in their particular area, and to put developing skills continually into practice.

On a general level, any course or training programme should cover the nature and purposes of oral communication – addressing the different approaches to be taken in different situations, and the techniques that can be used to communicate effectively.

In addition, there are many texts on the subject, allowing training to be complemented by structured reading. A good all-round text on communications is *Communications for Managers*, in the Practical Handbook series now managed by Capital Learning and Development (formerly the Industrial Society), and published in 1993. This incorporates a series of leaflets written for and produced by British Telecommunications employees, and covers a range of key communications issues. Remember that the final assessment interview includes a ten-minute presentation. This is therefore one of the easiest of the mandatory competencies for the panel to assess.

Practical guidance – communication skills

For Level 1 your candidate must be able to understand the various media in which written communications can be presented, and more importantly, the skills involved in doing so, with regard to the target audience, the length, style and layout of the communication, the message they wish to convey, and the structure of the communication. In terms of 'graphic' communication, it covers sketch notes, drawings in plans, designs linked to the construction process and similar (if these are relevant to the candidate's chosen pathway). It is probably easiest to assess understanding with reference to actual written work – their own and other peoples' – in a variety of mediums. They should consider why a particular communication fails or succeeds, how it could be improved, and what the aspects are that make it successful in a particular area.

For Level 2, put this knowledge into practice. Candidates need to consider a range of their written work, in a variety of media. Is it all appropriate for the audience and purpose? Have they achieved, in a letter, memo, report, e-mail, sketch or design what they set out to achieve? If they are experiencing difficulties in this area, they could attend a course (internal or external) on written communication. There are also a lot of useful books and texts on the subject, including The *Complete Plain Words*, by Sir Ernest Gowers and others, published by Stationery Office Books in 1986. Practice will again be key – nobody would expect them to write a perfect client report the first time they tried, but with a full understanding of the principles and purposes of the report, and some more practice, they will be much better equipped to do so.

The critical analysis submitted by your candidate for the final assessment provides an easy opportunity for the panel to assess the candidates' ability in this area.

Practical guidance – negotiation skills

This competency overlaps somewhat with the 'Conflict avoidance' competency, and my notes on that should prove useful here too.

To fulfil the requirements of this particular competency, check that your candidate understands what lies behind successful negotiations: the preparation of evidence; an understanding of the various approaches to negotiations; a knowledge of where and how parameters are set; a knowledge of what each side wishes to get from the negotiations, and from any future relationship; and so on. If possible, involve your candidate in negotiations. This is perhaps the best way of helping them to gain an understanding of principles and skills.

HEALTH AND SAFETY

Details of this competency are set out on page 31 of the *APC/ATC requirements and competencies guide*. For the purposes of recording in your candidate's achievement record, this competency has been given the reference M008. It is required to level 2.

The basic Level 1 requirement is to demonstrate a knowledge and understanding of the principles and responsibilities with regard to health and safety imposed by law; and codes of practice and other regulations relating to health and safety appropriate to your candidate's area of practice. This competency must be taken to level 2 where they will be required to provide evidence of practical application of health and safety issues and the requirements for compliance, in your candidate's area of practice.

Practical guidance

This competency covers all aspects of a surveyor's working life. It is about ensuring that the surveyor's entire working life is conducted as safely as possible with as little risk to health as possible, and that the same is true for all of those around the surveyor. It is easy to think of ways in which health and safety issues relate to, say, work on a construction site, but perhaps less so for more office-based work. However, the same basic philosophies underpin all work carried out in any environment. In off-site jobs, the issues encompass such things as managers knowing where a candidate is and what they are doing at all times, and, should they leave the office, when they will return and who they are meeting. There are also numerous health and safety issues relating to the use of equipment, in offices as well as all other locations, and on keeping employees healthy and safe.

Owing to the importance of health and safety, most firms and organisations conduct formal training and instruction on the relevant issues. Ensure that your candidate attends this and that they can explain the reasons behind any requirements imposed by the firm.

I would also recommend some general reading. The Health and Safety Executive (HSE) provides numerous free leaflets on its website, at www.hse.gov.uk, including lists of its current publications. You should encourage your candidate to visit the site and select some useful reading.

Finally, they must be able to demonstrate knowledge of the health and safety legislation and codes of practice that apply to their area of work, and also evidence of practical application as required by Level 2 of the competence. This will differ from one pathway to another, but includes such things as the *Health and Safety at Work Act* 1974, the *Construction (Design and*

Management) Regulations 1994 and the *Control of Asbestos at Work Regulations* 2002. Candidates must be aware of relevant legislation and able to explain it and its significance to their area of work.

ACCOUNTING PRINCIPLES AND PROCEDURES

Details of this competency are set out on page 29 of the *APC/ATC requirements and competencies guide*. For the purposes of recording in the candidate's achievement record, this competency has been given the reference M001.

This competency must be achieved to Level 1. The requirement is to demonstrate knowledge and understanding of fundamental accounting concepts; and the format and preparation of management and company accounts, including profit and loss statements, cash flow statements and balance sheets.

Practical guidance

Your candidate will undoubtedly be able to gain some experience – practical or theoretical – of these concepts in the course of their work. If there is one particular aspect that is unlikely to arise in their everyday work, consider how training might be arranged so that this is covered. If this proves impossible you should encourage your candidate to read a textbook on the subject, or attend an appropriate training course or CPD lecture.

It should be noted that some candidates might quite easily reach Levels 2 and 3 in this competency if this subject is part of their job. For example, a rural practice candidate working for an estate would deal with these types of issues regularly. Candidates working in commercial property and dealing, perhaps, with the leisure and entertainments industry, might also easily attain Level 2 or 3 through practical experience.

BUSINESS PLANNING

Details of this competency are set out on page 29 of the *APC/ATC requirements and competencies guide*. For the purposes of recording in the candidate's achievement record, this competency has been given the reference M002.

This competency must be achieved to Level 1. The requirement is to demonstrate knowledge and understanding of how business management activities contribute to the achievement of corporate objectives.

Practical guidance

This is a vast subject, and I would certainly advise that your candidate attend some kind of basic management training course, where possible. These are run by a number of bodies, including the Open University and the Chartered Management Institute. The candidate may well not be directly involved in managing your business, and this is not expected of them for the purposes of Level 1, but they must be able to understand – and explain to the assessors, if necessary – the underlying factors of business management.

A lot will also be learned on the job, of course, and coaching and training from you will be invaluable. There is a lot of overlap with the requirements of the other mandatory competencies (communications and negotiation, team-working, client care, and so on). I would also recommend that the candidate read a management skills textbook to develop knowledge and understanding of issues such as motivation, mission statements, strategy, organisational structures, and so on.

A useful text book in this respect is *The handbook of management and leadership a guide to managing for results* by Michael Armstrong and Tina Stephens published by London Kogan Page 2005 (ISBN 0 74944 34 48). This book covers the practice of management, delivering change, enhancing customer relations and enabling continuous improvement.

CONFLICT AVOIDANCE, MANAGEMENT AND DISPUTE RESOLUTION PROCEDURES

Details of this competency are set out on page 30 of the *APC/ATC requirements and competencies guide*. This competency has been given the reference M006 for the purposes of recording in the candidate's achievement record.

This competency must be achieved to Level 1. This requires knowledge and understanding of the techniques for conflict avoidance, conflict management and dispute resolution procedures, including for example adjudication and arbitration appropriate to your candidate's APC pathway.

Practical guidance

The 'ingredients' of this competency will vary greatly between the various faculty pathways. In commercial practice, for example, landlord and tenant matters will be fairly common, while in construction, this competency will be present everyday in managing building contracts. Indeed, in the Quantity surveying and Construction Pathway, this becomes a core competency to Level 2, with requirements based around procurement and the drafting of terms and conditions of leases, contracts and agreements.

In basic terms, and across all pathways, it is important that the candidate understands how to conduct negotiations, and also the various options available should negotiations break down, working through mediation and conciliation, adjudication, arbitration, independent expert determination, and, finally, litigation.

Candidates should be encouraged to sit in on negotiations at their firm from an early stage in their career. Also they will benefit from some formal training on this and other aspects of dispute resolution, covering the preparation of evidence, case law, approaches and tactics. It is reasonably likely that by the time they reach the final assessment, candidates will need to have had practical experience of running their own negotiations, or participating in other dispute resolution procedures, and will thus be able to discuss this. As part of their training plan ensure that they make steady progress towards this end.

There are also many texts available on this subject. To get started, I would recommend reading one or more of the following RICS guidance notes and practice statements:

- *Surveyors Acting as Arbitrators and as Independent Experts in Commercial Property Rent Reviews*

- *Surveyors Acting as Adjudicators in the Construction Industry*

- *Surveyors Acting as Expert Witnesses*

- *Chartered Surveyors Acting as Advocates*

All of these publications are available in hardcopy from www.ricsbooks.com (RICS members can download the publications as a PDF from www.rics.org). In addition, don't forget CPD-type lectures or training that may be available within the firm, or from external providers.

DATA MANAGEMENT

Details of this competency are set out in page 30 of the *APC/ATC requirements and competencies guide*. For the purposes of recording in the candidate's achievement record, this competency has been given the reference M007.

This competency must be achieved to Level 1. It involves demonstrating knowledge and understanding of the sources of information and data applicable to the candidate's area of practice, including the methodologies and techniques most appropriate to collect, collate and store data.

Practical guidance

Again, this competency will vary greatly between the APC pathways. It is important to think of it in relation to the candidate's specific route, and against the backdrop of their day-to-day work and the particular IT developments in their area.

In the Valuation pathway, for example, this competency will cover comparable evidence found in sales and rental evidence. Collection, collation and storage methods in this pathway will usually comprise the use of IT spreadsheets and databases, either developed by firms or sold as commercial packages. Developments in this area, and in the Commercial property pathway, include the use of CAMA (Computer Assisted Mass Appraisal) techniques.

In the Quantity Surveying and Construction pathway, meanwhile, sources of data may be previous contracts or cost guides and price books. Various commercial packages are also available to price contracts and bills of quantities. For all pathways, the important thing is for the candidate to be able to understand the use of data in their day-to-day work – how this is gathered and put to use, and what the best methods of collection, collation and storage are. Candidates should be able to step back mentally from their work, to explain what data they use, how they find it and how it is manipulated.

You should avoid the temptation to 'write this competency off', on the basis that it will be covered at Level 1 elsewhere – for example, in Level 1 of the Valuation competency. Try to use the competency to broaden and develop the candidate's understanding of wider data issues and developments in the profession. See this competency as a subject in itself and ensure your candidate carries out some structured reading. Discuss it as a discrete issue at some point in their training plan and at the three- and six-monthly review stages.

SUSTAINABILITY

Details of this competency are set out on page 31 of the *APC/ATC requirements and competencies guide*. For the purposes of recording in the candidate's achievement record, this competency has been given the reference M009.

As a mandatory competency this is required to level 1. It requires a knowledge and understanding of why and how sustainability seeks to balance economic, environmental and social objectives at, local, national and global levels, in the context of land, property and the built environment.

Practical guidance

All chartered surveyors need a basic understanding of environmental issues, which range from groundwater pollution and contaminated land, to control of pollution in the air we breathe, and on to even wider global issues, such as climate change. Environmental issues affect building design, construction use and management, development and re-development, and regeneration and town planning. Issues such as global warming, dwindling national resources and atmospheric pollutants are top priorities with many government and influential bodies, such as the EU and the World Trade Organisation (WTO).

I would suggest your candidate should carry out some general reading in newspapers and professional journals on environmental issues. Other useful sources of information and advice are the RICS guidance notes *Contamination and Environmental issues – their implications for property professionals and Asbestos and its implications for members and their clients.*

In addition, of course, candidates should maintain an awareness of environmental issues whilst at work. Candidates should be aware of any government initiatives, laws or EU regulations affecting their particular area of work. On a more local level, they should be aware of any internal office environmental policies (recycling of paper, for example), and be able to explain the purposes of these. You may like to test their knowledge and understanding in this area by asking them to consider how they would express the firm's 'green credentials', should this be requested in, for example, an invitation to tender. Once more, this is a case of stepping back from day-to-day work, for them to consider the environmental factors that underlie and overarch such work.

TEAM-WORKING

Details of this competency are set out on page 31 of the *APC/ATC requirements and competencies guide*. For the purposes of recording in the candidate's achievement record, this competency has been given the reference M010.

This competency is required to Level 1. Candidates must demonstrate a knowledge and understanding of the principles, behaviour and dynamics of team-working.

Practical guidance

This competency involves understanding why people work in teams, and some of the basic principles underlying team-working. In practice, candidates will rarely not work within a team, so in effect, while the mandatory requirement is to Level 1, in practice they will often be working to Level 2 ('working as a team member in a work or business environment').

Evidence of working in a team will be easy to come by – however, the Level 1 requirement is to understand the principles behind this. Candidates should therefore consider a situation in which they have witnessed or experienced team-working, and to explain how that team worked, concentrating on the roles each member adopted and the success or otherwise of this.

Candidates understanding can be complemented and extended by some reading on the subject. A leading text on this subject is *Management teams: Why they succeed or fail*, by R. M. Belbin, published by Butterworth-Heinemann in 2003.

A last word of advice

Hopefully you now have a better idea of what the mandatory competencies entail, and of how to help your candidate achieve them. Remember that the philosophies behind the mandatory competencies, and the business skills inherent in them, will be encountered in every aspect of their working life. It is for this reason that they are mandatory.

8. Referred candidates and appeals

We come now to the very last stage in the APC process. Your candidate has attended the final assessment interview and is waiting for the decision.

The assessment panel will make a decision as to whether your candidate has passed or failed within 24 hours of the interview. Normally, the outcome will then be notified to the candidate within 21 days. If the result is a pass, then all is well and good, and you can skip the rest of this chapter. If, however, the outcome is a referral (fail), the notification will include a 'referral report', which will give guidance as to why the panel has reached this decision.

Referral will be a miserable experience for the candidate, and it is important that the supervisor is on hand to provide help. In the first instance you will need to provide support by acting (in the usual sense of the word) as a 'counsellor', and may therefore wish to arrange a meeting with the candidate. In preparation for this, ask the candidate to write a few notes to reflect his or her memory of the experience, with reference to the contents of the referral report.

At the meeting, the first thing you will need to do is let the candidate 'get it off their chest'. You should sit back and listen, adopt an understanding tone and offer some words of comfort and a shoulder to cry on. When the more emotional stage is over, ask the candidate to discuss how he or she feels about the outcome, and centre your discussion on the referral report, checking the candidate's understanding of the reality of the situation. At all times remain realistic – at the end of the meeting you will be looking to agree one of two outcomes: to make an appeal, or to live with the referral and apply to take the final assessment again.

You should strive to achieve an outcome in which your candidate accepts responsibility for the situation, regardless of whether you intend making an appeal. This should provide a positive way forward for all concerned and put your candidate in the right frame of mind for the future – a win-win situation all round.

If you feel the referral is justified, then it is time to start planning how to succeed next time. If, however, the candidate wishes to make an appeal, then he or she has ten working days (from the date the result is posted by RICS) to do so.

Details of how to make an appeal are available on www.rics.org. Broadly speaking, appeals may be made on one of three grounds:

- administrative or procedural: the panel may not have been provided with the correct information or detail;

- the questioning and testing of competence concentrated too heavily outside of the candidate's main areas of training and experience; or

- any form of discrimination.

In most instances, no appeal will be lodged. The next step for the supervisor is therefore to steer the candidate through (at least) a further six months of training and to make preparations for the next assessment.

There are some minimum requirements that referred candidates must satisfy. They must:

- record a minimum of a further 100 days of relevant professional experience. (The assessors will probably give some guidance as to which particular areas to concentrate on);

- undertake a minimum of a further 24 hours of professional development;

- write a new critical analysis; or if recommended by the assessors, resubmit the original, suitably amended, with updates;

- agree with the supervisor and counsellor how the deficiencies identified in the referral report will be addressed; and

- submit the final assessment record giving details of the further 100 days of training and experience in relation to the competencies.

Another Supervisor's and counsellor's report will also need to be completed for the additional training period.

The advice given previously in this book on filling in Summaries of progress, forward plans, and supervisor's and counsellor's reports hold good for Template 10 (the Declaration of completion of referral assessment). See Chapter 4 for more information on filling in such forms.

At the end of the six months, or later, if the candidate has deferred further, the candidate will be re-interviewed. This will take the same format as the original interview, including a presentation on the relevant critical analysis.

It is of course important that the supervisor and counsellor continue to provide support and encouragement over the six-month period. You will be involved in planning the additional training) and, in assisting the candidate to fill in Template 9 the referral record. You will need to carry out another six-monthly-style review, checking all relevant documentation.

At the end of the period you will also have to complete Template 10 – the Declaration of Completion of Interim Assessment, which confirms your candidate's readiness for reassessment.

WHAT WENT WRONG – AND HOW DO WE PUT IT RIGHT?

At this stage, what both the candidate and the supervisor and counsellor want to know is 'what went wrong' the first time round? Knowing this, they can endeavour to put it right for the next time. Most referred candidates pass at the second attempt – making it clear that there is a simple way of adjusting or adding to performance, to ensure success.

Having said that, there is no magic formula to achieve a pass at the second attempt. However, the following examples indicate where a concentration of effort in one particular area may be the key to success. The referral report will of course indicate which specific aspects should be considered.

Sometimes, there is something very concrete and easy to put right. Often, this relates to the critical analysis. Go back to my discussion of this on page 69, and, in conjunction with the comments in the referral report, make sure that the new report submitted matches all the requirements.

Another omission that, in a final assessment situation, can be thought of as 'instant death', is a lack of knowledge of the Rules of Conduct. Make sure your candidate has a good knowledge of these for their second attempt – see page 91 for full advice on these.

Sometimes, the first failure was just about under-preparation in general, often in combination with over-confidence. Go back over the stages in this book, test, and retest the candidate on the competencies, and have them re-present their presentation to you and another colleague. Make sure they know everything back to front. Check also that they have a good, wider knowledge of each area, and have not simply learnt something verbatim, leaving them unable to explain the principles or processes behind an action. For example, I remember one referred candidate commented that he carried out a certain type of valuation calculation by simply inputting two numbers into an Excel spreadsheet and pressing a button to get the answer. While this may be standard practice, the candidate needed – and failed – to understand the processes behind the 'magic' calculation.

On other occasions, a candidate may simply have given a poor performance on the day. Ask them to undergo a mock interview with you, or another supervisor or colleague. Assess their performance under pressure, and consider how it could be improved.

Sometimes, the candidate has just had back luck – with particular problems hard to define. Often, the solution in these instances is simply to undertake a little more training and experience.

In the experience of senior assessors, the 'reasons for referral' can be broken down roughly as follows. Some 85% of candidates fail simply because they are not 'competent'. As noted above, to achieve competency, it is often just a matter of improving experience and knowledge in one particular area; a lack of competency at this stage is by no means an indication that competency will never be achieved. The referral report will indicate any particular areas of weakness to focus on.

Another 10% of candidates are referred because they fail to demonstrate competency. Their critical analysis may have been weak, their presentation poor, or the examples they produced to support their achievements poorly thought through. If you know your candidate is competent, but if he or she failed to get this across at the interview, then consider, using the referral report, how he or she can better demonstrate competency in the problematic areas.

The final 5% fail for a variety of reasons: by making simple mistakes on the day, often caused by a bad case of nerves; by making mistakes in the submitted documents (which checking and double-checking can avoid); or as a result of other, usually avoidable problems, which are unlikely to be repeated a second time round.

With the pass rate for second attempts at the APC so high, candidates should certainly not despair. Neither should their supervisors or counsellors. A little more time and effort is almost always all that is required.

A final word of advice

Having helped one particular referred candidate to subsequent success, supervisors and counsellors should take some time to consider whether the lessons learnt could be applied to other candidates in the system.

Help and advice from RICS

I hope that this book has given you an insight into the importance of your role as a supervisor or counsellor – and sufficient advice on how to carry it out. The roles carry with them a great deal of responsibility. However, you are not alone.

Working in conjunction with the faculties and the Education and Membership Committee, RICS, has set up extensive helpline facilities for candidates and employers. The following points of assistance can help with any of the aspects of your role outlined in this book.

- RICS Contact Centre + 44 (0)870 333 1600

- RICS website: www.rics.org

- Regional representatives (the RICS regional teams often organise training sessions for APC candidates. Contact details for regional administrators can be obtained from RICS at the above telephone number)

- RICS training advisers (RTAs – see below)

- APC doctors (see below)

Remember too, that advice is provided in the official RICS guides: the *APC candidate's guide*, the *APC/ATC requirements and competencies guide*, the *APC guide for supervisors, counsellors and employers* and the *APC*

Pathway Guides. The RICS Books publication, *APC 2006 – your practical guide to success*, will also prove useful.

RICS TRAINING ADVISERS

RICS employs 12 training advisers in the UK. Details may be found on the RICS website, at www.rics.org.

The role of the RTAs is to advise firms on all aspects of the APC. Most importantly, they are able to help firms develop 'approved' structured training agreements for candidates (see Chapter 5 for more information on these). In drawing up such an agreement, the RTA will provide initial advice to the firm. When the firm has prepared a training agreement that meets with the minimum standards described in Chapter 5, it will be deemed 'approved'. It may then be used as an indicator of excellence and of the firm's commitment to APC training – which may prove very useful in job advertisements and at recruitment fairs.

Over the years RTAs have built up a wealth of knowledge and understanding of APC training across the APC pathways. As such, they are an excellent source of guidance and knowledge. My advice is quite simple – use them.

APC DOCTORS

Whereas the primary role of the RTAs is to support and advise employers, voluntary APC doctors are available to assist and guide candidates through the system. They are normally locally based and, where practical, will be from the same faculty as the candidate's chosen route. They are often recently successful APC candidates and can therefore provide others with the benefit of their first-hand experience. Details of local APC doctors can be found on www.rics.org.

READING MATERIAL

All of the guidance notes and practice statements noted in this book can be obtained from www.ricsbooks.com. RICS Books can likewise assist with the ordering of the other publications listed in this book. APC candidates may find particularly useful the RICS online suite of publications – isurv (www.isurvlive.co.uk). The isurv 'channels' cover a huge range of surveying topics, mixing expert commentary with official RICS guidance.

OTHER MATERIAL

Jon Lever, FRICS, an RTA, has developed a 'timeline wallchart' for the APC, presenting a pictorial view of the process. This can be ordered free of charge from DeLever Limited, at www.delever.co.uk.

Conclusion

The candidates that arrive at your firm are your raw material. You, the supervisors and counsellors, must shape them into future surveyors. It can seem a daunting task. Hopefully, the advice in this book, and the additional guidance and support available from RICS, will ensure that you feel comfortable in carrying out that task successfully.

I would like to leave you with some final words of advice – illustrated by examples I have encountered over the years.

Respect the individuality and diversity of your candidates. Do not expect candidates to be the mirror image of yourself – or imagine that this would necessarily be a good thing! I remember one supervisor (a very experienced surveyor) who became incensed by his candidate's poor grasp of written English (which obviously limited that candidate in terms of the mandatory competency of communication and negotiation – not to mention in other areas). In truth, the candidate was perfectly well able to express himself in writing, but had a much lower standard of spelling and grammatical correctness than the supervisor was accustomed to. The counsellor, with the ability to take an overview of the situation, encouraged the candidate to enrol on a basic course to improve his written skills. He also pointed out to the supervisor that the candidate was extremely proficient at other forms of communication – particularly with regard to information technology. In fact, the candidate was some way ahead of both the supervisor and counsellor in respect of his knowledge and experience in this area.

Remember also that different candidates require different approaches. If a project has not gone too well, a straightforward approach, with (constructive) criticism, may work for some people. For others, you may have to employ a greater level of tact. If you take the time to get to know your candidates, you will soon understand which approach works best for them.

Keep your candidate, and his or her progress, constantly in your mind. Do not think of the APC process as something to dip in and out of at specified intervals. Rather, you should be always on the look-out for opportunities for your candidate, chances to resolve difficulties, and prospects for the future.

In one large firm, a supervisor became aware of major negotiations taking place in another department. Aware that her candidate could gain much from these, she persuaded her colleagues to allow the candidate to sit in on these, at a much earlier stage in his career than would otherwise have been the case.

Far and away the most common call for help to RICS comes from candidates who feel that their supervisors and counsellors are not spending enough time with them, or taking enough of an interest in their progress. There is obviously a simple answer to such problems – spending more time, or, if this is not possible, communicating the reasons for this to the candidate. The following example illustrates this:

In early 2004 a candidate phoned RICS to make the above complaint, noting that he felt his employer was in breach of the firm's structured training agreement. A candidate on the construction pathway, he was spending too much time on the measurement and costing of construction works, but gaining no experience in contract practice. Discussions with an RICS training adviser (RTA) and his supervisor and counsellor revealed that the firm he was working at had just been awarded a large contract, which had made it essential for the candidate's time to be concentrated in one particular area. This situation was due to change in a matter of months, at which point the candidate's experience in contracts would be widened. Clearly, had this been appropriately communicated to the candidate, the problem would not have arisen in the first place.

Understand the importance of 'standing back'. To be able to identify your candidates' achievements against the competencies, you need to have the ability to stand back from their day-to-day work, and consider how the requirements of the competencies are reflected in that. This will help you explain how to fill in the various records of progress, thinking of each day's work in terms of its constituent factors. You should also encourage your candidate to acquire the same skill of 'standing back', so that they can answer unexpected questions at the final assessment interview. Candidates who understand the principles and processes behind everything they do will be able to answer any question that is thrown at them.

Avoid the 'halo and horns' effect, which refers to what happens when objectivity gets lost. If you have had a good experience with a candidate, you may be ready to believe the best of them in all situations, and may avoid pointing out failings, preferring not to mention these. After a bad experience, on the other hand, it can be easy to view a candidate over-critically. The two experiences often go hand in hand, with one candidate appearing to do no wrong, and another appearing to do no good. Strive hard to resist either extreme. Make sure you look objectively at your candidates' work, and seek confirmation of your judgments from other colleagues.

Act professionally at all times. You are of course steering your candidates through a process in which they must learn to abide by the RICS code of ethics and Rules of Conduct. Throughout the training process you will be a walking, living example of these Rules in practice. You must therefore act professionally towards your candidates at all times, leading by example.

Do not put undue pressure on your candidate to take the final assessment. I have encountered candidates who have felt ready to take their final assessment some time before their supervisors and counsellors have concurred in this belief. Conversely, I have met candidates with such an overwhelming sense of personal modesty that, had it not been for the supervisor insisting on them taking the assessment, would still be training several years later! Accept that people progress at different speeds. The worst thing that can occur is to enter an under-prepared candidate for the final assessment. The subsequent referral gets the candidate's career off to a bad start, and makes everyone feel dissatisfied. Two years is a minimum target – there is no shame in taking longer.

If your candidate is not ready for the assessment (even if he or she thinks they are), or alternatively, if you feel they are ready, but they think otherwise, then listen to them, and consider how you can reach an agreed state of readiness. You may wish to arrange a meeting, at which strengths and any 'under-developed strengths' can be identified, and a clear timetable drawn up, indicating how skills will be gained. Clarity should provide confidence.

Seek advice if problems arise which you feel you cannot resolve. This is particularly pertinent if problems arise in which you yourself are involved. We are only human – it is not unknown for relationships to break down on occasion. In these circumstances, act carefully and thoughtfully. Have you contributed, in any sense, to the breakdown or difficulties? How could you modify your approach or behaviour? Seek advice from your peers who may have encountered similar situations or alternatively discuss the matter with a senior colleagues (where relevant you could also try the Membership Operations Department of RICS).

Above all, remember that as a supervisor or counsellor, you have someone looking up to you, requiring your guidance and expertise. Take your responsibilities seriously; follow the advice in this book, and you will be very well-equipped to guide your candidate to success!

Index